Helping Vulnerable Youths

Runaway & Homeless Adolescents in the United States

Deborah Bass
Principal Investigator

Project Staff
Leila Whiting, *Project Manager*
Doreta Richards, *Project Coordinator*
Leann Crook, *Administrative Assistant*

NASW PRESS

Barbara White, PhD, ACSW
NASW President

Mark G. Battle, ACSW
NASW Executive Director

Prepared with support from the U.S. Department of Health and Human Services; Administration on Children, Youth, and Families; and Family and Youth Services Bureau Grant #90CK 2124.

First impression July 1992
Second impression April 1994

Library of Congress Cataloging-in-Publication Data

Bass, Deborah S.
    Helping vulnerable youths : runaway & homeless adolescents in the
United States / Deborah Bass, principal investigator ; project
staff: Leila Whiting, project manager, Doreta Richards, project
coordinator, Leann Crook, administrative assistant.
      p.   cm.
    "Prepared with support from the U.S. Dept. of HHS; Administration
on Children Youth & Families; and Family and Youth Services Bureau-
-Grant #90Ck2124."
    Includes bibliographical references and index.
    ISBN 0-87101-221-9
    1. Social work with youth--United States. 2. Runaway teenagers-
-Services for--United States.   3. Homeless youth--Services for-
-United States.   I. National Association of Social Workers.
II. Title.
HV1431.B38   1992
362.7'4--dc20   92-21848
                                        CIP

Printed in the United States of America

Cover and interior design by Susan Marsh

This monograph does not necessarily represent the views of the U.S. Department of Health and Human Services.

NASW Communications Staff

Linda Beebe
Associate Executive Director, Communications Division

Lucy Sanchez
Director, News and Media Production

Nancy Winchester
Managing Editor, Books and Journals

Demonstration Site Staff

From the Juvenile Welfare Board of Pinellas County, Florida

James Mills
Executive Director

Lynn Hildebrand
Project Manager

From Family Resources, Inc., Pinellas County, Florida

Lois Martin
Outreach Worker

Stuart Nussbaum
Director of Residential Services

Art O'Hara
Assistant Director

Theartis Scott
Outreach Worker

From the University of South Florida, Florida Mental Health Institute, Jacksonville

Karl Achenbach
Evaluator

Technical Advisory Panel

Marion F. Avarista
Executive Director
Travelers Aid of Rhode Island

Edward Bradford
Senior Program Analyst
Administration for Children, Youth, and Families
Family and Youth Services Bureau

Della M. Hughes
Executive Director
The National Network of Runaway and Youth Services, Inc.

Gail L. Kurtz
Executive Director
Southeastern Network of Youth and Family Services

James Mills
Executive Director
Juvenile Welfare Board of Pinellas County, Florida

Carol Smith
Director
School of Social Work and Attendance
School Board of Broward County, Florida

Federal Project Office

Kaaren Gaines Turner
Project Officer

Contents

Foreword

As individual social workers, we have a responsibility to advocate on behalf of vulnerable clients and for services that will be effective in improving their lives. As an association, the National Association of Social Workers (NASW) has a dual responsibility: to the clients and to the social work practitioners who work with them. NASW supports advocacy efforts by individuals and works to develop policy and program recommendations based on sound information. We know that policymakers need clear information on the causes of problems and potentially successful remedies to create effective programs. Effectiveness must be measured both in how well programs alleviate problems and in how cost-effective they are. In a time of resource constraints, we cannot afford to squander our capital on programs that do not resolve the problems they are supposed to address.

NASW's concern about developing appropriate social policies and programs led to the creation of the National Center for Social Policy & Practice in 1986. Since that time, the National Center has built a solid research library with special information resources and topical databases. Each year, the center provides practice and policy information to hundreds of practitioners and policymakers.

Helping Vulnerable Youths: Runaway & Homeless Adolescents in the United States is another step in NASW's efforts to produce better information about the problems of society and the needs of practitioners. NASW is happy to have this opportunity to contribute to the development of informed policies and practices. We appreciate the support of the U.S. Department of Health and Human Services for the project that resulted in this monograph.

The youths of our nation represent our future. Yet, all too many youths see no future for themselves. *Helping Vulnerable Youths* looks at the problems and abuses that lead youths to run away or become homeless, at the programs designed to help them, and at the policy issues concerned. Based on the first nationwide survey of service providers who serve runaway and homeless youths in more than a decade, the monograph reveals some staggering data. Many of our youths have been so battered by their parents or by society that they require extensive help to become competent and contributing members of our society. If we are to deliver that help sufficiently, we must resolve a number of policy issues. The last chapter of *Helping Vulnerable Youths* reviews those issues and suggests research, training, and policies that could improve our ability to help runaway and homeless youths.

I highly recommend this monograph to you. In addition to the Department of Health and Human Services, NASW would like to thank the Demonstration Site Staff from the Juvenile Board of Pinellas County, Florida; Family Resources, Inc., of Pinellas County; and the University of South Florida, Florida Mental Health Institute, Jacksonville, as well as the Technical Advisory Panel. (See pages iii–iv for a list of people that includes the staff who worked hard to produce this resource.) Most especially, I would like to thank Deborah Bass, who served as Principal Investigator, author, and creator of this project.

MARK G. BATTLE, ACSW
Executive Director, NASW

June 1992

Introduction

Youths in the United States face many serious problems, including family problems and difficulties created by society. They have high incarceration rates, especially among minorities. Suicide is the second leading cause of death among young people from 15 to 24 years of age. Many youths are victims of physical or sexual abuse by parents and other family members. Drug and alcohol abuse continue to be serious problems. During the year 1985, 41 percent of high school seniors used marijuana and 13 percent used cocaine (U.S. Department of Education, 1986).

Runaway and homeless youths each year in the United States number approximately 1.2 million to 1.5 million (Systemetrics/McGraw-Hill, 1989, p. 31). These numbers do not include the many youths who run away from foster care or residential placements. More than one out of five runaway and homeless youths seeking shelter, however, are running away from foster or group-home care. Thirty-eight percent of the runaway and homeless youths seeking shelter have been in foster care at some time during the previous year. Many runaway and homeless youths have been abused and are considered "behaviorally disturbed," suicidal, or violent. Their numbers include youths who have voluntarily chosen to leave their parental homes and those who have no homes to which they can return.

The youths who run away from home, those who run away from foster care, and those who are homeless often go to special youth shelters. Many of these community-based shelters receive part of their funding from the U.S. Department of Health and Human Services. Since 1988, shelters that receive some federal funds have reported serving approximately 63,000 youths annually—only a fraction of those who need services. Many of the youths who need such help are unaware that it is available, and some are afraid that if they seek help they will be returned to a family that is abusive or that has serious problems. Other youths may receive services from state or locally funded shelters and services, although no documentation of this is available.

States responding to the 1991 survey of the National Association of Social Workers on the needs of runaway and homeless youths and the programs available to help them. (Shaded states responded.)

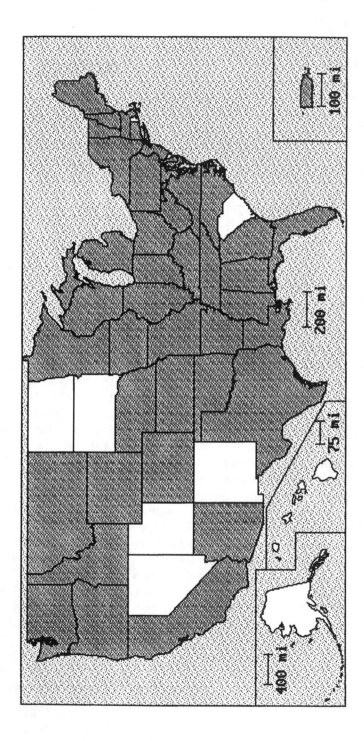

To develop practice-relevant information and to identify innovative practices, the National Association of Social Workers (NASW) undertook the project that resulted in this monograph. With support from the Family and Youth Services Bureau of the Administration on Children, Youth, and Families in the U.S. Department of Health and Human Services, NASW examined the needs of runaway and homeless youths and the programs available to help them. Between January and April of 1991, NASW surveyed 360 agencies that provide basic shelter and crisis intervention services and transitional living services to runaway and homeless youths. It also surveyed state coordinators of independent living services. The NASW survey results provide information about the state of services and practices for runaway, homeless, and other needy youths.

NASW received excellent response to its 1991 survey. As the map accompanying this Introduction shows, providers in all but 10 of the 54 states and territories responded. (See Appendix A for a full description of the survey instrument and methodology.)

Unfortunately, the survey results are disheartening with regard to the problems facing America's youth. Abuse, parental substance abuse, and many other problems affect most runaway or homeless young people.

Despite the enormous problems facing youths, however, service providers are trying to meet their needs and are offering an exhaustive array of services. NASW assembled a panel of experts to review these services and to identify the best practices, based on the survey data and on the panel's knowledge about and experience with youths. The Juvenile Welfare Board of Pinellas County, Florida, agreed to demonstrate the resulting comprehensive model of service delivery to test the validity of the model. This monograph is based on the survey results, on the model developed by experts, and on the continuing demonstration experience.

Many social workers are employed in shelters and other community-based programs for youth. Through the publication of this monograph, NASW hopes to provide practical information to them and to other youth workers employed in programs that serve some of the nation's neediest young people.

References

Systemetrics/McGraw-Hill. (August 1989). *A partial listing of problems facing American children, youth and families.* (Prepared for the Office of the Assistant Secretary for Planning and Evaluation, U.S. Department of Health and Human Services). Lexington, MA: Author.

U.S. Department of Education. (1986). *What works: Schools without drugs.* Unpublished manuscript.

Executive Summary

This Executive Summary highlights the results of two nationwide surveys conducted by NASW between January and April of 1991 with support from the U.S. Department of Health and Human Services (HHS). NASW surveyed 360 agencies that provide basic shelter, crisis intervention services, and transitional living services to runaway and homeless youths and 51 state coordinators of the Social Security Act's Title IV-E independent living services. The findings of the surveys were used to identify best practices. The Juvenile Welfare Board of Pinellas County, Florida, agreed to demonstrate some of these practices.

WHO ARE RUNAWAY AND HOMELESS YOUTHS?

There are no "typical" runaway or homeless youths. They come from a variety of backgrounds and environments. Some have been forced out of their family homes; some have run away from their homes. Others have run away from juvenile institutions or from residential facilities or foster homes. Still others just want to escape parental control temporarily.

Despite differences in background and environment, however, these youths share many of the same family problems. Many have experienced physical and sexual abuse, parental drug and alcohol abuse, and other violence in the family setting.

The nationwide NASW survey confirms what other, smaller studies have suggested—that large numbers of these youths are not short-term runaways. The survey shows that more than one out of five youths who arrived at shelters were coming directly from foster or group homes, and 38 percent had been in foster care at some time during the previous year. Eleven percent arrived at shelters from other runaway or crisis shelters, and 11 percent had been on the street before coming to the shelters. Fifty percent returned to their parental or guardian's home following shelter care. Thus, many of the runaway and homeless youths throughout the country have long-term problems that may preclude their returning to a family setting. It appears that prior services have not helped these youths resolve their problems.

As indicated above, these youths leave their homes or legal residences because of severe problems. The NASW survey shows that more than 60 percent of the youths in shelters and transitional living facilities nationwide had been physically or sexually abused by parents, and 26 percent had experienced violence from other family members. This finding is not surprising—the *National Incidence Study* (U.S. Department of Health and Human Services, 1981) showed that one out of four known child abuse cases involves a 12- to 17-year-old. Abuse of adolescents is often undetected until they come in contact with professionals such as child protective services workers, staff of shelters for runaways, or juvenile court personnel (Straus, 1990).

Many parents of runaway and homeless youths are substance abusers. The NASW survey shows that parents of 29 percent of the youths had problems with alcohol, and parents of 24 percent were drug abusers. In fact, most of the service providers responding to the survey reported that parental substance abuse was a problem. Furthermore, several studies suggest that parental consumption of alcohol has a direct relation to adolescent alcohol consumption (Barnes, 1990).

The NASW survey data reveal other national trends, including these:

- 83 percent of the 169 programs responding to the survey receive client referrals from law enforcement agencies, and 75 percent receive referrals from the juvenile justice system;
- 27 percent of the clients of the respondent programs were in trouble with the justice system.

Shelters may have cultivated relations with the justice and law enforcement systems to encourage such referrals. The high percentage of these referrals suggests, however, that the youths may not have received services that could have prevented their involvement with those systems.

According to the survey, the average length of shelter stay and aftercare for almost half the youths is more than one month. The seriousness of the problems they face suggests that they will need long-term assistance to overcome the problems or, for older youths, to learn to live independently.

Some of the problems of runaway and homeless youths mirror the problems of American society. Shelter providers responding to the NASW survey reported that 41 percent of their clients were from families with long-term economic problems. Close to half were from households with absent fathers. More than one-third of the youths had no means of support. Consistent with the generally excessive high school dropout rates for these youths, more than half had serious educational or school problems.

The factors just described as influencing runaway and substance-abusing behavior highlight some of the most significant problems facing these youths and their families. Even more revealing are the providers' responses to the NASW survey question about the problems their youth clients had experienced (see Table ES-1). According to the providers, more than 50 percent of the youths had more than one of the problems listed in the table.

PROGRAMS DESIGNED TO HELP NEEDY YOUTHS

The first program to depart from traditional ways of reacting to troubled youths—that is, by not treating them all as delinquents—was the Runaway Youth Program established by Congress in 1974. (The law establishing this program was later amended to include homeless youths.) The purpose of the program is to supplement services provided by the juvenile justice system and the child welfare system by offering short-term crisis intervention to youths who have *not* been placed in shelters by courts. Congressional expectations

Table ES-1. Problems Facing Runaway and Homeless Youths

Problems Faced by Youth Clients	Percentage of Youth Clients with Problem
Education/school problems	53
Absence of father	45
Family with long-term economic problems	41
Youth was in foster care	38
Other [than sexual] abuse of youth by parent	38
Youth has no means of support	37
Parent is an alcoholic	29
Youth is in trouble with justice system	27
Youth has mental health problem	26
Violence by other family members [i.e., other than parent]	26
Parent is a drug abuser	24
Sexual abuse by parent	23
Youth is drug abuser	23
Absence of caretaker	23
Youth has attempted suicide	20
Youth is an alcoholic	19
Parent has mental health problem	18

SOURCE: National Association of Social Workers, 1991 Survey Examining Needs of Runaway and Homeless Youths and Programs Available to Help Them (1991 Runaway and Homeless Youth Survey). See Appendixes A and B in this monograph for Description of the NASW Survey and Analysis of Findings, and State Summaries of Provider Responses, respectively.

were that the program would alleviate the problems of these young people, reunite them with their families, help them resolve intrafamily problems, strengthen family relationships, and stabilize living conditions.

The U.S. Department of Health and Human Services interpreted short-term care to mean no more than 15 days of care in a shelter setting. This 15-day limitation on the length of temporary stay keeps the focus on crisis intervention. Thus, shelters provide a safe place for the young person to eat and sleep, and shelter staff contact the youth's family to try to achieve family reunification.

Despite the 15-day limitation, the shelters provide an exhaustive array of services that are designed to help the youths resolve current crises and prevent future ones. The 24 services offered by at least 75 percent of the providers responding to the NASW survey are listed in Table ES-2.

Table ES-2. Services Provided by Most Respondents to NASW Survey

Service	Percentage of Shelters Providing Service
Information and referral	98
Provide individual counseling	98
Screening/intake	96
Temporary shelter	95
Case management	94
Refer to drug abuse program	94
Provide meals	93
Coordinate with juvenile justice system	93
Provide family counseling	92
Refer for mental health services	90
Outreach	89
Refer for health care	89
Refer for treatment for suicidal behavior	89
Provide recreational program	87
Provide advocacy for clients	87
Refer to program for alcoholics	86
Refer for other living arrangements	82
Refer to educational program/GED	82
Refer to family counseling	81
Refer for individual counseling	79
Provide AIDS/HIV education	78
Follow-up to referral	77
Provide aftercare services	76
Provide transportation	75

SOURCE: NASW, 1991 Runaway and Homeless Youth Survey.

Legislation for the Runaway Youth Program also required that shelters receiving federal funds develop an adequate plan for aftercare counseling for each youth and his or her family. As shelter staff discovered the tremendous needs of the youths seeking their help, they not only found more providers to whom they could refer youths, but they began to provide more aftercare services themselves. The NASW survey showed that 76 percent of the providers said that they offer aftercare. When asked about specific aftercare services, however, 96 percent said that they provide services when the youths leave their shelters. Table ES-3 lists aftercare services offered by at least 66 percent of the providers that responded to the survey.

Recognizing that older homeless youths are less likely to be reunited with their families and that runaways with serious problems need more intensive help, Congress created the Transitional Living Program for homeless youths. This program was designed to meet the broader societal and environmental needs of youths. It is expected that youths leaving the program will have acquired skills in obtaining a job, housing, and access to needed services.

Although 68 percent of all respondents to the NASW survey reported that they refer youths to transitional living services, only 32 percent actually provide those services themselves. However, the number of providers offering transitional living services is growing; 39 providers have added these services since their programs began.

Although more youths for whom independent/transitional living would be appropriate are now moving into such programs, unfortunately because of limited resources many others are not. Some of the latter are returning to the street; many are entering or returning to foster or group-home care. Table ES-4 shows survey results with regard to destinations of young clients on leaving the shelters.

Table ES-3. Aftercare Services Provided by Most Respondents

Aftercare Service	Percentage of Shelters Providing Service
Individual counseling	93
Family counseling	88
Case management	82
Counseling for drug abuse	77
Group counseling	75
Counseling for alcoholism	74
Parent counseling	72
Mental health services	69

Source: NASW, 1991 Runaway and Homeless Youth Survey.

Table ES-4. Program Impact on Youths Ready for Independent Living

Destination	Average Percentage of All Youth Clients	Average Percentage of Youth Clients Ready for Independent Living
Parent's/guardian's home	51	32
Home of other parent figure	9	15
Relative's home	8	15
Foster home	12	19
Group home	10	16
Independent/transitional living	8	29
Back to the street	8	18

SOURCE: NASW, 1991 Runaway and Homeless Youth Survey.
NOTE: Percentages are averages and therefore do not total 100.

The staffing of shelters and transitional living programs reflects the providers' understanding of the serious long-term problems facing youths who seek their help. The percentages of survey respondents who use professional staff are shown in Table ES-5. Clearly, providers believe that they must have some professionally trained staff in their programs.

YOUTHS IN FOSTER CARE INDEPENDENT LIVING PROGRAMS AND THE SERVICES THEY RECEIVE

NASW received 14 responses from the 51 state independent living coordinators surveyed (a 28 percent response rate). Three other states provided

Table ES-5. Professional Staff Employed by Providers Responding to Survey

Profession	Percentage of Providers Employing	Average Percentage of All Employed Staff
BA in social work	74	17
BA in psychology	66	18
BA in counseling	36	9
MSW	61	12
MA in psychology	39	7
MA in counseling	54	11

SOURCE: NASW, 1991 Runaway and Homeless Youth Survey.

information about their programs although they did not complete the survey form.

The Independent Living Program was designed to serve youths who have been in foster care but are not runaways. As noted earlier, however, there appears to be considerable overlap in the two populations, as evidenced by the fact that 38 percent of the runaways seen in shelters have been in foster care during the previous year. Some states recognize this overlap. One state, New York, for example, requires that a youth 16 years of age or older only reside in care for at least 12 months within the preceding 36 months. That same child could have been a runaway before or after he or she entered care.

A comparison of the primary services offered by the providers who responded to the questionnaire on runaway and homeless youth with the services offered by the state independent living programs (for those responding) show a few significant differences. Far more (100 percent) of the independent living programs provide a program for alcoholics than do the programs for runaway and homeless youths (18 percent). As expected, far more of the independent living programs also help youths develop independent living plans (100 percent versus 70 percent), provide training in independent living skills (100 percent versus 63 percent), and refer youths for employment assistance (93 percent versus 71 percent).

Very few of the aftercare services provided by these two types of programs are similar. Both provide case management and mental health services, but the aftercare programs for runaway and homeless youths focus on counseling for the individual, family, and parent; group counseling; and counseling for substance abuse problems. Independent living aftercare programs focus more on "hard" services such as education, job training, employment, health care, and financial assistance.

These differences between the independent living programs and the basic center and transitional living programs may not, however, result in significant differences for the youths who receive help from them. The destinations of youths in independent living programs are remarkably similar to those of runaway and homeless youths who are ready for independent living, although fewer independent living program clients than transitional living clients return to the streets.

A "MODEL" PROGRAM

A "model" program should represent the best of current practices rather than an ideal program that many providers might not be able to achieve. A "model" should describe not only desired outcomes but also a process that is necessary before providers can implement the "best" practices for their own areas. Following is a brief description of the model proposed by NASW following the nationwide survey. The Juvenile Welfare Board of Pinellas County, Florida, and Family Resources, Inc., a local agency that serves youths, are demonstrating parts of the model.

Key Components in NASW's Comprehensive Model of Service Delivery for Runaway and Homeless Youths

Identify education, health, and social service systems. This stage includes determining how to access key personnel, obtain appropriate referrals, and develop cooperative agreements for joint service responsibilities. The joint service responsibilities should include shared case information, joint case planning, and joint follow-up and use of resources.

Develop and implement outreach activities with target populations. Outreach must establish informal, one-on-one, direct contact with youths wherever they are. Typical target populations for outreach are street youths, youth clients in other public and private agencies or in schools and community centers, youths in "hot" spots such as malls and fast food places, and minority and immigrant youths.

Develop and implement public awareness activities. Public awareness activities should reach civic groups, religious groups, media, professional organizations, funders, public policy bodies, religious organizations, fraternal and civil rights organizations, advocacy organizations, and community and neighborhood groups.

Empower youths and families in the development, implementation, and evaluation of services. A model program should involve youths and their families in cooperative case planning, peer support and educational groups, outreach and public awareness, agency and community policymaking, experiential sharing, and advocacy.

Develop and implement initial and ongoing assessment tools and mechanisms to identify clients' needs, problems, resources, and progress. Providers should develop, modify, or use a screening/intake tool, an assessment tool, a protocol for the assessment process to ensure its quality, a substance abuse protocol jointly developed by the youth shelter and a substance abuse program, and an individual case plan and contracting agreement with the client.

Develop outcome measures and follow-up of service plan to completion or assess clients' achievement at three-, six-, and 12-month intervals. Because aftercare is an important part of shelter activities, it is important to continue to assess progress toward achieving and maintaining the goals of the case plan and to refine the plan as necessary.

Advocate for quality, client-centered policies, programs, and services for youths and families. The provider's ability to serve youths depends on the availability of services. For this reason providers have a responsibility to develop an advocacy plan for developing and maintaining needed services in the community.

Develop and implement coordinated programwide and ongoing staff training programs. Training for new staff and volunteers and ongoing training on emerging trends is important.

References

Barnes, G. M. (1990). Impact of the family on adolescent drinking patterns. In R. L. Collins, K. E. Leonard, & J. S. Searles (Eds.), *Alcohol and the family* (pp. 137–161). New York: Guilford Press.

Straus, M. (1990). *Abuse and victimization across the life span.* Baltimore: Johns Hopkins University Press.

U.S. Department of Health and Human Services, National Center on Child Abuse and Neglect. (1981). *National incidence study.* Washington, DC: U.S. Government Printing Office.

1 Characteristics and Needs of Vulnerable Youths

How is it that some youths in the United States find themselves in situations where the fear of living on the streets is less menacing than the fear of remaining in their own homes? Why are so many youths in trouble with the law? How can professionals help them resolve the problems that resulted in these situations?

Some of the neediest youths in the United States are those who already are or who are at risk of becoming status offenders. Juvenile status offenders are youths under 18 years of age who are charged with offenses such as curfew violation, truancy, possession of alcohol, and running away (U.S. General Accounting Office, 1991). They can be held in secure detention facilities for these offenses, although the United States has made a concerted effort to prevent such detention.

This chapter examines the characteristics and status of homeless youths and youths who have been served by programs designed to prevent their detention. These vulnerable youths face many problems that lead not only to status offenses but also to poor quality of life and little potential for future achievement. The problems faced by runaway and homeless youths are so severe that living on the streets is preferable to living at home. Table 1 shows the similarity in risk factors for runaway behavior, for placement in foster care, and for drug and alcohol abuse. Younger children who are at risk may receive help from child protective services and may be placed in foster care. Older children who are at risk are more likely to run away, or to become substance abusers, or both.

Some factors identified in Table 1—abuse, poor achievement in school, and parental substance abuse—can result in low self-esteem. Low self-esteem may lead to runaway behavior and substance abuse, resulting in even lower self-esteem.

1

Table 1. Common Risk Factors for Troubled Children and Youths

Risk Factors Contributing to Foster Care Placement (Metropolitan Washington Council of Governments, 1991)	Risk Factors for Runaway Behavior (NASW Survey)	Risk Factors for Drug and Alcohol Abuse (Kurtz, Jarvis, & Kurtz, 1991)
Neglect	Neglect	
Abuse	Abuse	Abuse
Parental substance abuse	Parental substance abuse	Parental substance abuse
Mental health problems of child or parent	Emotional conflict	Family conflict
Lack of parenting skills		Poor parenting skills
Child substance abuse	Child substance abuse	
Child behavior problems	Poor school performance, low self-esteem	Poor school performance, low self-esteem

WHO ARE RUNAWAY AND HOMELESS YOUTHS?

As mentioned, there are no "typical" runaway or homeless youths. They come from a variety of backgrounds and environments. Some have been forced out of their homes; some are chronic runaways from their family homes. Others have run away from juvenile institutions or from residential facilities or foster homes. Still others just want to escape parental control temporarily.

The U.S. Department of Health and Human Services (1989) defines runaway and homeless youth as follows:

- A runaway is a youth away from home at least overnight without the permission of his or her parent(s) or legal guardian; and
- A homeless youth is one who has no place of shelter and is in need of services and a shelter where he or she can receive supervision and care.

Recent work (Kurtz, Jarvis, & Kurtz, 1991) further defined homeless youths according to five types of problems that might have caused their homelessness:

1. Youths who already are members of homeless families and become separated from those families
2. Youths who leave home to escape physical and sexual abuse
3. Youths who are thrown out of their homes by parents or guardians
4. Youths who were removed from or thrown out of their family homes and then ran away from intolerable placements
5. Minority youths who immigrated unaccompanied to the United States

SIMILARITIES IN PROBLEMS FACED BY RUNAWAY AND HOMELESS YOUTHS

The Office of Substance Abuse Prevention in the Department of Health and Human Services identified three types of factors that influence alcohol and other drug use. Those factors have been modified here to provide a social work perspective. The four factors, from that perspective, are interpersonal relationships, societal influences, personal factors, and environmental factors. Figure 1 shows the relations among these factors.

Interpersonal Relationships

This discussion of factors that influence runaway and substance-abusing behavior among youths begins with their interpersonal relationships because children and youths depend heavily on their parents. Other relationships with authority figures are also important.

As mentioned, despite differences in background and environment, runaway and homeless youths share many of the same family problems, including physical and sexual abuse, parental drug and alcohol abuse, and other violence in the family setting.

The nationwide NASW survey confirms what other, smaller studies have suggested—that large numbers of these youths are not short-term runaways. A New York State Task Force on the Homeless (New York State Council on Children and Families, 1984) found that nearly 60 percent of the youth sampled entered shelters from foster care or from mental health or juvenile justice systems. The study also concluded that 64 percent of the short-term runaways needed alternative placements because returning to their homes would put them in danger.

The NASW survey shows that more than one out of five youths who arrived at shelters were coming directly from foster or group homes; 38 percent of the youths had been in foster care at some time during the previous year. Eleven percent arrived at shelters from other runaway or crisis shelters, and 11 percent had been on the street before coming to the shelters. Fifty percent returned to their parental or guardian's home following shelter care. As these figures show, many of the runaway and homeless youths throughout the country have long-term problems that may preclude their returning to a family setting. It appears that prior services have not helped these youths resolve their problems.

As indicated above, these youths leave their homes or legal residences because of severe problems. A study of "street youth" in Denver, Colorado (Oleson, 1986), revealed that 85 percent of the study population reported

Figure 1. Factors influencing runaway and substance-abusing behavior. SOURCE: Taken, in part, from U.S. Department of Health and Human Services (1990).

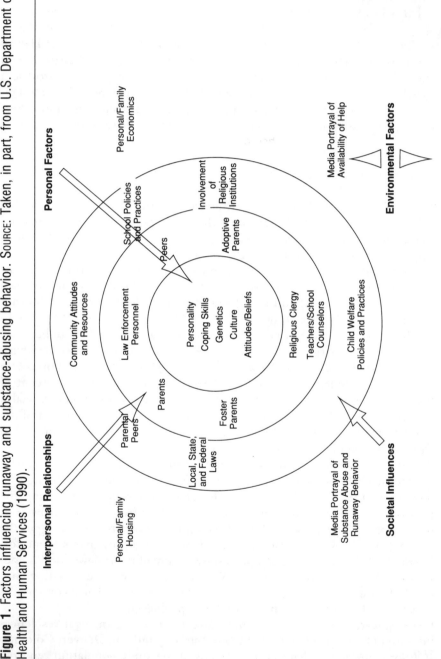

sexual or physical abuse in their homes before they departed. The NASW survey shows that more than 60 percent of the youths in shelters and transitional living facilities nationwide had been physically or sexually abused by parents. In some states, however, the percentage of youths who had been abused by parents appears to be much higher. (See Appendix B for state summaries of provider responses.) For example, California providers reported that 39 percent of their clients had been sexually abused by a parent and 57 percent had suffered other types of abuse from a parent. Texas providers reported that 37 percent of their clients had been sexually abused by a parent and 56 percent had been otherwise abused by a parent.

The NASW survey shows that one out of four youths in shelters and transitional living facilities nationwide had experienced violence from family members other than parents. This is not surprising—the *National Incidence Study* (U.S. Department of Health and Human Services, 1981) showed that one out of four known child abuse cases involves a 12- to 17-year-old. Abuse of adolescents is often undetected until they come in contact with professionals such as child protective services workers, staff of shelters for runaways, or juvenile court personnel (Straus, 1990).

According to a young author who came through the Canadian child welfare system (Raychaba, 1988), problems of abuse are often further exacerbated by the child welfare system. According to this author, who drew on U.S. and Canadian child welfare literature and personal experience, many youths in foster care are maltreated by foster parents. A recent article in *Child Welfare* (Carbino, 1991) suggested that 1/2 to 1 percent of all reports to governmental authorities of abuse involve foster parents. These figures may be low. Raychaba (1988, p. 32) maintained that more than half of the children abused in foster care were not abused in their own homes. No data are available, however, on the extent to which abuse occurs in foster care and other residential settings. Short-term shelter care cannot help young people come to terms with problems resulting from abuse.

Many parents of runaway and homeless youths are substance abusers. The NASW survey shows that parents of 29 percent of the youths had problems with alcohol, and 24 percent were drug abusers. Recent studies have shown that parental substance abuse continues to be a problem for runaway and homeless youths. A 1976 study funding by the National Institute on Alcohol Abuse and Alcoholism revealed that runaways reported parental alcohol abuse as the second most important reason for running away (Van Houten & Golembiewski, 1978). In response to the NASW survey, most of the service providers reported that parental substance abuse was a problem. Several studies suggest that parental consumption of alcohol has a direct relationship to adolescent alcohol consumption (Barnes, 1990). Providers in some states with large populations under age 18 believe

Table 2. Average Percentage of Youths in Three Large States Whose Parents Abuse Substances

	California $n = 16$[a]	Texas $n = 7$[a]	Florida $n = 15$[a]
Parents abuse alcohol	35%	36%	32%
Parents abuse drugs	29%	24%	26%

[a] Number of shelter and transitional living providers responding in state.
Source: Appendix B in this monograph.

that more of the parents of their youth clients have substance abuse problems than the national figures suggest (Table 2).

Societal Influences

The NASW survey data reveal other national trends, including these:

- 83 percent of the 169 programs responding to the survey receive client referrals from law enforcement agencies, and 75 percent receive referrals from the juvenile justice system;
- 27 percent of the clients of the respondent programs were in trouble with the justice system.

Shelters may have cultivated relations with the justice and law enforcement systems to encourage such referrals. The high percentage of these referrals suggests, however, that the youths may not have received services that could have prevented their involvement with those systems. Straus (1990) cited one study that concluded that between 40 and 90 percent of youths in trouble with the law have been repeatedly or brutally abused.

A recent study conducted for the Office of Juvenile Justice and Delinquency Prevention (U.S. Department of Justice, Office of Juvenile Justice and Delinquency Prevention, 1990) on runaways surveyed juvenile residential facilities. Of the facilities that agreed to participate in the survey, group foster homes reported the most frequent runaways. Many youths also ran away from residential treatment centers. Few runaways were from mental health facilities, juvenile detention centers, medical hospitals, schools for the disabled, and boarding schools.

The significance of prior experience in foster care or group-home care cannot be overstated. Raychaba (1988) cited a study that suggests that at least one out of five of these youths will eventually be dependent on welfare. He also cited studies of the New York Runaway and Homeless Youth Advocacy Project and of the National Youth Bureau in England that show that youths coming out of care are more likely to become homeless. (As do the NASW survey data, the New York study showed that one out of four runaway and homeless youths had been in care [Raychaba, 1988]).

Raychaba, an ex-ward of the Catholic Children's Aid Society of Metropolitan Toronto, succinctly summarized the impact of prior care:

> The general transience and residential instability of many youth out of care is [sic] the end result of various threads which, when amassed together, can be said to constitute the social and psychological tapestry of the after-care experience. Their generally poor economic situation, isolation from positive social support networks, and their lingering and unaddressed psychological and emotional difficulties are all facets of this reality. Many likely come to work in unskilled and inadequately-paying forms of employment due to their lack of schooling and occupational training as well as their deficiencies of work-related social skills. Frequent residence change is also likely associated with a lack of money management skills needed to balance budgets and pay bills. Besides mental health problems which many of these youth carry with them from care, the negative aspects of emancipation—feelings of abandonment, loneliness, and isolation—also make for a situation in which simply coping is difficult enough. (Raychaba, 1988, pp. 65, 66, 67)

Personal Factors

Runaway and homeless youths have many personal problems and self-damaging behaviors that they must change if they are to improve the quality of their lives. Parental substance abuse is a recognized risk factor for such problems among the children of these parents. Thus, it is not surprising that the NASW survey reveals that 19 percent of the youths abused alcohol and 23 percent abused other drugs.

The problems facing runaway and homeless youth constitute risk factors for many of their self-damaging behaviors and poor family relationships. The damaging behaviors in turn become risk factors for further problems and additional damaging behavior. The self-damaging behaviors, or personal factors, of older youths who have been abused may include eating disorders, self-abuse, nervous disorders, lack of motivation, depression, withdrawal, poor grades, and alcohol and drug abuse (Raychaba, 1988, p. 30). These behaviors may also include delinquency, running away, truancy, schizophrenia, prostitution, teen pregnancy, and suicide (Straus, 1990).

Service providers reported to NASW that almost a quarter of the run-away and homeless youths have mental health problems; 20 percent of them have attempted suicide. This nationwide information confirms the serious problems raised in a recent report of the U.S. General Accounting Office (1989), which showed that about three out of five of these youths suffer from depression and about 10 percent are considered suicidal. Raychaba (1988) suggested that

> youth in care and youth out of care are not two distinct creatures; many of the characteristics and problems of the former are often retained by the latter. . . . The problems they deal with related to inner emotional difficulties, depression, anxiety, as well as possible drug and alcohol abuse most likely persist and become compounded. In many ways, therefore, the condition of youth in contact with child welfare is prone to steady deterioration once care is terminated. (pp. 65, 66, 67)

For almost half the youths, the average length of shelter stay and after-care is more than one month, according to the NASW survey. The serious-ness of the problems they face suggests that they will need long-term assistance both to overcome the problems or, for older youths, to learn to live independently. Those who have been away from home for some time have more severe health needs than do their peers. They are likely to experience the results of poor nutrition, inadequate hygiene, respiratory diseases, drug and alcohol abuse, physical and sexual victimization, and unwanted pregnancies. Their more frequent involvement in sexual activity increases their risk of contracting AIDS/HIV infection (U.S. General Accounting Office, 1989).

Environmental Factors

Some of the problems of runaway and homeless youths mirror the prob-lems of American society. Shelter providers reported to NASW that 41 percent of their clients were from families with long-term economic prob-lems. Close to half were from households with absent fathers. About one-third of the youths had no means of support. Consistent with generally excessive high school dropout rates, more than half had serious educational or school problems.

The factors just discussed as influencing runaway and substance-abusing behavior highlight some of the most significant problems facing these youths and their families. Even more revealing are the providers' responses to the NASW survey question about the problems their youth clients had experienced (see Table 3). According to the providers, more than 50 percent of the youths had more than one of the problems listed in the table.

The problems listed in Table 3 are categorized in Table 4 according to the type of factor influencing the problem or behavior. It is revealing that the primary environmental influence listed in Table 5 is the inability of the youth or family to provide economic support for themselves. As shown in Table 4, the top three problems that youths experience affect their economic well-being. Education/school problems affect the youth's long-term earning capabilities. If parents have to take time off from work to deal with these problems, their earning capacity is also affected. It is also well documented that families suffer financially when the father is absent. Yet this is a problem affecting almost half of the runaway and homeless youths seen by providers who responded to the NASW survey. When families have had long-term economic problems, it is more difficult to regain a solid economic status.

Three societal systems have a significant influence on the youths, their families, and their ability to cope with their problems—the school system,

Table 3. Problems Facing Runaway and Homeless Youths

Problems Faced by Youth Clients	Percentage of Youth Clients with Problem
Education/school problems	53
Absence of father	45
Family with long-term economic problems	41
Youth was in foster care	38
Other [than sexual] abuse of youth by parent	38
Youth has no means of support	37
Parent is an alcoholic	29
Youth is in trouble with justice system	27
Youth has mental health problem	26
Violence by other family members [i.e., other than parent]	26
Parent is a drug abuser	24
Sexual abuse by parent	23
Youth is drug abuser	23
Absence of caretaker	23
Youth has attempted suicide	20
Youth is an alcoholic	19
Parent has mental health problem	18

SOURCE: National Association of Social Workers, 1991 Survey Examining Needs of Runaway and Homeless Youths and Programs Available to Help Them (1991 Runaway and Homeless Youth Survey). See Appendixes A and B in this monograph for Description of the NASW Survey and Analysis of Findings, and State Summaries of Provider Responses, respectively.

Table 4. Factors in Youth's Background Influencing Alcohol or Drug Abuse

Personal Factors	Interpersonal Factors	Societal Influences	Environmental Factors
Education/school problems	Sexual abuse by parent	Education/school problems	Family has long-term economic problems.
Youth has mental health problem.	Other abuse by parent		
	Violence by other family members	Youth is in trouble with the justice system.	Youth has no means of support.
Youth is drug abuser.	Parent is an alcoholic.	Youth was in foster care.	
Youth has attempted suicide.	Parent is a drug abuser.		
	Absence of father		
Youth is an alcoholic.	Absence of caretaker		

the juvenile justice system, and the child welfare system. Yet none of these systems has resolved many of the youths' problems.

Runaway and homeless youths often face problems over which they have no control. These problems are summarized in Table 5. The only problems for which these young people can take action or try to learn coping skills are the abuse and the parental substance abuse.

REDEFINING SUCCESS FOR YOUTHS WITH LONG-TERM PROBLEMS

Much has been written about the need to educate runaway and homeless youths about the risk of AIDS and its relation to drug abuse. Service providers have very little opportunity, however, to change the high-risk behavior of youths in the short period of time that they are at a shelter. Many youths do not value their own lives. A grant from the Administration

Table 5. Typical Problems Faced by Runaway and Homeless Youths over Which They Have No Control

Abuse
Parental substance abuse
Long-term economic problems
Failure of service systems to help them resolve problems
Limited potential for future independence and improved quality of life without significant support and interventions

on Children, Youth, and Families (ACYF) to Children's Hospital in Los Angeles included a survey of runaway service agencies (Children's Hospital, Los Angeles, 1988). The purpose of the survey was to identify educational activities on AIDS prevention. All of the agencies reported that adolescents' feelings of immortality, fear of authority figures, and sense of hopelessness made AIDS insignificant to them. Thus the agencies were uncertain about the impact of their educational efforts.

One shelter provider received a "high-impact" grant from ACYF that was designed to provide alternative services to some of these youths (Youth & Shelter Services, unpublished report). The project targeted youths who had run away three or more times for extended periods and older homeless adolescents. The provider's evaluation report stated that success for youths with serious long-term problems must be measured in a different way from that of success for youths who do not have these problems. According to this provider, few of its youth clients successfully moved to an independent living situation, but many were able to survive without returning to the streets. One example was a client who did not get a GED or a full-time job but was able to maintain a part-time job and did not return to the streets.

Although the National Institute on Drug Abuse believes that drug abuse research has identified behavioral, biomedical, and neurobiological factors involved in drug abuse, knowledge about the effectiveness of existing drug treatments is limited (U.S. General Accounting Office, 1990). It is especially important to determine what strategies work with runaway and homeless youths. Of the providers responding to NASW's survey, 94 percent reported that they refer youths to drug abuse programs, and others actually provide such a program.

It is clear that an effective program for runaway and homeless youths must help these young people deal with the totality of their needs and problems. This means that social workers and other service providers must not only help youths deal with the problems they face, but they also must help youths and their families build on existing strengths. Resiliency factors cited by the Southeastern Network (Jarvis, 1990) included these:

- four or fewer children, spaced more than two years apart
- much attention paid to infant during first year
- positive parent–child relationship in early childhood
- additional caregivers besides mother
- care by siblings and grandparents
- steady employment of mother outside of household
- availability of kin and neighbors for emotional support
- structure and rules in household
- shared values

- close peer friends
- availability of counsel by teachers and/or ministers
- access to special services (health, education, social services)

When youths have access to support systems, and when family members have had to learn coping and problem-solving skills, they are more likely to have skills and strengths upon which they can draw. The problems become much more difficult to resolve when the service systems (for example, access to special services) and environmental supports (such as steady employment) are not available. When the supports are not available, service providers must develop services and encourage other types of community response to the problems facing runaway and homeless youths and their families.

A strong case can be made for preventive programs so that youths are not compelled to run away or become homeless. The remainder of this monograph, however, deals with ways to help those who have not had the benefit of such programs.

References

Barnes, G. M. (1990). Impact of the family on adolescent drinking patterns. In R. L. Collis, K. E. Leonard, & J. S. Searles (Eds.), *Alcohol and the family* (pp. 137–161). New York: Guilford Press.

Carbino, R. (1991). Advocacy for foster families in the United States facing child abuse allegations: How social agencies and foster parents are responding to the problem. *Child Welfare, 70*(2), 131–149.

Children's Hospital, Los Angeles. (1988). *High impact grant: Youth at Risk Diversion Program, quarterly report.* Unpublished report.

Finkelhor, D., Hotaling, G., & Sedlak, A. (May 1990). Runaways. In *Missing, abducted, and throwaway children in America: Numbers and characteristics* (NCJ No. 123667, pp. 171–225). Washington, DC: U.S. Department of Justice, Office of Juvenile Justice and Delinquency Prevention.

Jarvis, S. U. (1990). *Drug use among runaway and homeless youths: A southeastern perspective.* Athens, GA: Southeastern Network of Youth and Family Services.

Kurtz, D., Jarvis, S., & Kurtz, G. (1991). Problems of homeless youths: Empirical findings and human services issues. *Social Work, 36*(4), 309.

Metropolitan Washington Council of Governments. (1991). *Why are kids in foster care?* Washington, DC: Author.

New York State Council on Children and Families. (1984). *Meeting the needs of homeless youth* (Prepared by the Homeless Youth Steering Committee). Silver Spring, MD: National Association of Social Workers.

Oleson, J. (1986). *Treating street youth: Some observations.* Unpublished manuscript.

Raychaba, B. (1988). *To be on our own with no direction from home.* Ottawa, Ontario, Canada: National Youth in Care Network.

Straus, M. (1990). *Abuse and victimization across the life span.* Baltimore: Johns Hopkins University Press.

U.S. Department of Health and Human Services, Office of Substance Abuse Prevention. (1990). *Findings of the High-Risk Youth Demonstration Program. (Report No. 10). Learning about the effects of substance abuse prevention: A progress report.* Rockville, MD: Author.

U.S. Department of Health and Human Services. (1989). *Annual report to the Congress on the Runaway and Homeless Youth Program, fiscal year 1989.* Washington, DC: U.S. Department of Health and Human Services; Office of Human Development Services; Administration of Children, Youth, and Families; Family and Youth Services Bureau.

U.S. Department of Health and Human Services, National Center on Child Abuse and Neglect. (1981). *National incidence study.* Washington, DC: U.S. Government Printing Office.

U.S. General Accounting Office. (1989, December). *Homelessness: Homeless and runaway youth receiving services at federally funded shelters* (Report No. GAO/HRD-90-45). Washington, DC: General Accounting Office.

U.S. General Accounting Office. (1990, September). *Drug abuse research on treatment may not address current needs* (Report to the Chairman, Select Committee on Narcotics Abuse and Control, U.S. House of Representatives, Report No. GAO/HRD-90-114). Washington, DC: Author.

U.S. General Accounting Office Testimony (1991, May 22). *Noncriminal juveniles: Detentions have been reduced but better monitoring is needed* (Report No. GAO/T-GGD-91-30). Washington, DC: U.S. General Accounting Office.

Van Houten, T., & Golembiewski, G. (1978). *Adolescent life stress as a predictor of alcohol abuse and/or runaway behavior.* Washington, DC: American Youth Work Center.

Youth & Shelter Services. *Runaway, Homeless and Missing Youth Services Center High Impact Project evaluation.* Unpublished report.

2 Federal Programs Designed to Help Needy Youths

Several federal programs were designed specifically to help troubled youths. This chapter discusses the Runaway Youth Program (amended to include homeless youths), the Transitional Living Program, the Drug Abuse Education and Prevention Program, and the Independent Living Program.

RUNAWAY YOUTH PROGRAM

The first program to depart from traditional ways of reacting to troubled youths—that is, by not treating them all as status offenders or delinquents—was the Runaway Youth Program established by the Juvenile Justice and Delinquency Prevention Act of 1974 (P.L. 93-415). (This law was later amended to include homeless youths). The purpose of the program is to supplement services provided by the juvenile justice system and the child welfare system by offering short-term crisis intervention to youths who have not been placed in shelters by the courts.

Congress established the Juvenile Justice and Delinquency Prevention Act of 1974 because the number of juveniles leaving and remaining away from home was increasing. Although no data were available on exactly how many young people were running away, it was clear that more young people needed temporary shelter and counseling services. Law enforcement officials were finding it increasingly difficult to locate, detain, and return runaways. Congress believed that the federal government should establish a system for accurate reporting of the numbers of runaways and should help establish a system of temporary care outside the law enforcement structure because of the interstate nature of the problem.

Congress expected that the Runaway Youth Program would alleviate the problems of these youths, reunite them with their families, help them resolve intrafamily problems, strengthen family relationships, and stabilize living conditions.

The U.S. Department of Health and Human Services interpreted short-term care to mean no more than 15 days of care in a shelter setting. This 15-day limitation on the length of temporary stay helps keep the focus on crisis intervention. Thus, shelters provide a safe place for the young person to eat and sleep, and shelter staff contact the youth's family to try to achieve family reunification.

Despite the 15-day limitation on temporary stay in a shelter, the shelters provide an exhaustive array of services that are designed to help the youths resolve current crises, reunite them with their families, and prevent future crises. The 24 services offered by at least 75 percent of the providers responding to the NASW survey are listed in Table 6. Clearly, the providers believe

Table 6. Services Provided by Most Respondents to NASW Survey

Service	Percentage of Shelters Providing Service
Information and referral	98
Provide individual counseling	98
Screening/intake	96
Temporary shelter	95
Case management	94
Refer to drug abuse program	94
Provide meals	93
Coordinate with juvenile justice system	93
Provide family counseling	92
Refer for mental health services	90
Outreach	89
Refer for health care	89
Refer for treatment for suicidal behavior	89
Provide recreational program	87
Provide advocacy for clients	87
Refer to program for alcoholics	86
Refer for other living arrangements	82
Refer to educational program/GED	82
Refer to family counseling	81
Refer for individual counseling	79
Provide AIDS/HIV education	78
Follow-up to referral	77
Provide aftercare services	76
Provide transportation	75

Source: NASW, 1991 Runaway and Homeless Youth Survey.

that these services are essential if they are to help the types of youth who seek their assistance.

Legislation for the Runaway Youth Program also required that shelters receiving federal funds develop an adequate plan for aftercare counseling for each youth and his or her family. As shelter staff discovered the tremendous needs of the youths seeking their help, they not only found more providers to whom they could refer youths, but they also began to provide more aftercare services themselves. The NASW survey showed that 92 percent of the shelter and transitional living programs now identify specific services that they provide as part of aftercare. Table 7 lists aftercare services offered by at least two-thirds of the providers that responded to the survey. It is not surprising that most of the aftercare services are types of counseling, because the legislation mandates that these kinds of services be provided.

Short-term shelter services are extremely effective for youths who have been away from home for a short time and who seek help. Many youths do not seek them out, however. A recent study conducted for the Office of Juvenile Justice and Delinquency Prevention (U.S. Department of Justice, 1990) showed that only 2 percent of the runaways (using a somewhat narrow definition) spent any time at a runaway shelter and that at least 29 percent were without a familiar and secure place to stay. This suggests that many youths are unaware of the services available.

Short-term shelter services may not be as effective for youths who have long-term problems. Because shelters must move youths out after 15 days or terminate their participation if they do not follow shelter rules, some youths may not sustain their involvement in treatment. This means that

---

Table 7. Aftercare Services Provided by Most Respondents

Aftercare Service	Percentage of Shelters Providing Service
Individual counseling	93
Family counseling	88
Case management	82
Counseling for drug abuse	77
Group counseling	75
Counseling for alcoholism	74
Parent counseling	72
Mental health services	69

SOURCE: NASW, 1991 Runaway and Homeless Youth Survey.

they will need crisis intervention services again (Straus, 1990). Also, these services are designed to help youths with personal and interpersonal problems. They do not address the needs for other service systems or for improved living environments.

TRANSITIONAL LIVING PROGRAM

Recognizing that older homeless youths are less likely to be reunited with their families and that runaways with serious problems need more intensive help, Congress amended the Juvenile Justice and Delinquency Prevention Act of 1974 in 1988 to add the Transitional Living Program for homeless youths. Projects funded under the Transitional Living Program (Title III, Part B, Section 322a) are intended to

- provide supervised shelter with an adequate staff-to-client ratio in group homes, supervised apartments, host family homes, or similar facilities
- provide services that help youths achieve independence, such as information and counseling in basic life skills, interpersonal skill building, educational and vocational opportunities, and mental and physical health care
- develop an individualized, written transitional living plan that includes referrals and coordination of services with social services and law enforcement, educational, vocational training, legal, welfare, and health care services
- develop outreach programs to identify and recruit eligible youths.

This program was designed to meet the broader societal and environmental needs of youths, who are intended to leave the program with skills in obtaining a job, housing, and access to needed services.

DRUG ABUSE EDUCATION AND PREVENTION

Through the Omnibus Anti-Drug Abuse Act of 1988, Congress amended the Juvenile Justice and Delinquency Prevention Act of 1974 by adding the Drug Abuse Education and Prevention Program for Runaway and Homeless Youth. The purpose of the program is to fund demonstration and service delivery projects that support special drug abuse education and prevention programs for these young people. It supplements existing programs by providing additional funds to organizations such as shelter providers already serving the youths. The services funded through this program help organizations provide more of the longer-term aftercare services necessary to combat substance abuse—for example, individual, family, and group counseling; peer counseling; community education activities including outreach services; information and training; and improved coordination of local services.

INDEPENDENT LIVING PROGRAM

Congress established a program related to the Transitional Living Program—the Independent Living Program—as part of the Consolidated Omnibus Budget Reconciliation Act of 1985. This program authorizes grants to states for foster care children who are 16 or older. States must help these older foster care children make the transition to independent living through services such as counseling, training in daily living skills, and other services that can help them become self-sufficient. This program does *not* pay for residential or shelter services. Specific objectives of the Independent Living Program (U.S. Department of Health and Human Services, 1989, pp. 1–2) are to

- allow participants to work on a high school diploma, GED, or vocational training
- train youths in daily living skills, budgeting, locating and maintaining housing, and career planning;
- provide individual counseling, group counseling, and coordinate services for participants
- establish outreach programs designed to attract youths who are eligible for the program
- provide each participant with a written transitional independent living plan based on an assessment of need, which shall be incorporated into that youth's case plan
- provide participants with other services and assistance designed to improve their transition to independent living.

This program is also designed to equip youths with skills that will help them cope with societal and environmental factors.

Table 8 compares the objectives of the Basic Shelter, Transitional Living, and Independent Living programs for runaway and homeless youths. When the law creating them was enacted, the Independent Living and Transitional Living programs were designed to serve two different groups of youths. Both were aimed at helping older youths make the transition to independent living, but the Independent Living Program targeted those

Table 8. Summary of Distinctions among Programs Serving Runaway and Homeless Youths

Type of Grant	Authorization	Group of Youth	Restrictions	Provider Agency	Purpose	Specific Objectives for Youths
Basic Center	Juvenile and Delinquency Prevention Act of 1974, as amended (P.L. 96-509)	Runaway and homeless youth ages 12 to 18	15 days in shelter	Community-based agencies, primarily not-for-profit, can be for-profit	Short-term shelter and crisis intervention	1. Shelters in areas that can be reached easily by runaway and homeless youths 2. Contact with child's parents/ relatives to assure safe return or other arrangements 3. Plan for proper relations with law enforcement, social services, schools, welfare, corrections 4. Plan for aftercare counseling (for youths and their families)
Transitional Living	Juvenile and Delinquency Prevention Act of 1974, Part B, Section 321(a), (P.L. 100-690), as amended	Homeless youths aged 16 through 21	Up to 18 months of shelter; limit of 20 beds per program	Public or nonprofit organizations (group or family homes or other supervised residences)	Shelter and services to promote transition to self-sufficient living	1. Shelter 2. Services to increase independence 3. On-site supervision 4. Adequate staff-to-client ratio 5. Individualized transitional living plan 6. Outreach
Independent Living	Social Security Act, Title IV-E, Section 477, as amended; Consolidated Omnibus Budget Reconciliation Act of 1985	Youths aged 16 through 21	Youths either must be eligible for foster care under Title IV-E, or (at state option) must have been in foster care after their 16th birthday; does not include shelter	Federal funds go to state agencies, that in turn contract with public and private agencies	Services designed to promote transition from foster care to independent living	1. Assistance in getting high school diploma or equivalent 2. Training in daily living skills 3. Individual and group counseling 4. Coordinated services 5. Outreach 6. Individualized transitional independent living plan 7. Other services to improve transition to independent living

who had been in foster care, whereas the Transitional Living Program was devised to help older homeless youths who were in crisis and needed to learn to live independently. According to the NASW survey, however, 38 percent of the youths seeking help from shelters were in foster care during the previous year, so the programs may be serving many of the same youths. Although it is too early to assess the success of these programs, the NASW survey tried to capture changes that have resulted from them and to determine whether the programs were beginning to meet the long-term needs of youths.

CHANGES RESULTING FROM AVAILABILITY OF FUNDS TO ADDRESS SUBSTANCE ABUSE PROBLEMS

The Drug Abuse Education and Prevention Program for Runaway and Homeless Youth was designed to respond to the needs of increasing numbers of youths with substance abuse problems. Data from the NASW survey suggest that service providers have used the funds to expand their efforts to prevent and help youths overcome such problems. Table 9 shows the key services added by providers during the past five years that may help youths with substance abuse problems.

When asked how important specific services were to their ability to intervene or prevent substance abuse, providers identified the services shown in Table 10 as those that they both provide often and consider very important. Continued work with the individual and family ranked high, as did the need for careful screening when a youth enters a program.

Table 9. Key Services Added by Providers

Service	Percentage of Programs Adding Service
Drug abuse program	33
Referral to drug abuse program	21
Program for alcoholics	15
Referral to program for alcoholics	18
Family counseling	20
Aftercare	24

SOURCE: NASW, 1991 Runaway and Homeless Youth Survey.

Table 10. Services Rated as Most Important by Providers

Service	Percentage of Providers Offering Service	Percentage of Providers Considering Service Very Important
Individual counseling	98	89
Screening/intake	96	87
Refer to drug abuse program	94	85
Provide family counseling	92	89
Refer to program for alcoholics	86	79
Refer to family counseling	81	76
Refer for individual counseling	79	76

Source: NASW, 1991 Runaway and Homeless Youth Survey.

Changes Resulting from Availability of Funds for Longer-Term Programs

Respondents to the NASW survey included 23 service providers in 16 states that had received Transitional Living Grants (see Figure 2). Two-thirds of all respondents said that they refer youths to transitional living. Only one-third actually provided transitional living services, but more than two-thirds helped youths develop independent living plans. Providers that helped youths develop such plans helped them plan to meet future needs and find resources even if the providers did not offer transitional housing. Without the transitional living/housing services, providers may not be able to make available the long-term assistance and follow-up that many of the youths need. The number of providers offering transitional living services is growing, however: 39 providers have added transitional living services since their programs began, 45 programs added independent living skills training, and 32 providers added aftercare to their programs. In addition to the youths helped by these added services, many more need such help.

To assess whether the availability of funds for transitional living services affected what happened to youths when they left a program, the NASW survey asked providers about the destination of all youth clients and *the destination of youth clients for whom independent/transitional living would be appropriate.* Some of the responses (adjusted to reflect a national estimate) are shown in Table 11.

Although more youths for whom independent/transitional living would be appropriate are now moving into such programs, unfortunately many others are not. Some of the latter are returning to the street; many are

Figure 2. States with service providers that were Transitional Living Grant recipients responding to the NASW survey. (Shaded states responded.)

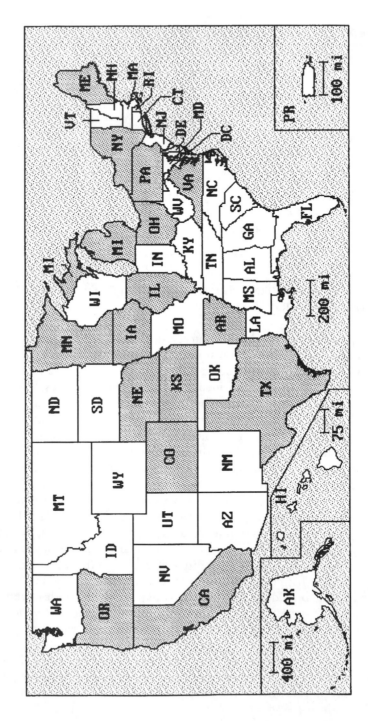

Table 11. Program Impact on Youths Ready for Independent Living

Destination	Average Percentage of All Youth Clients	Average Percentage of Youth Clients Ready for Independent Living	Percentage of Independent Living Clients
Parent's/guardian's home	51	32	30
Home of other parent figure	9	15	11
Relative's home	8	15	11
Foster home	12	19	14
Group home	10	16	14
Independent/transitional living	8	29	27
Back to the street	8	18	8

Note: Statistics on the independent living program clients were reported by state-level coordinators; the other data were obtained directly from providers.
Source: NASW, 1991 Runaway and Homeless Youth Survey.

entering or returning to foster or group home care. Far fewer are returning to their parents' or guardians' homes.

CHANGES RESULTING FROM AVAILABILITY OF FUNDS FOR INDEPENDENT LIVING PROGRAMS

Respondents to the survey of independent living coordinators (see Appendix C) included 14 (out of 51) states, or 28 percent. Three other states provided information about their programs, although they did not complete the survey form. Because the large states (for example, New York, California, and Texas) did not respond to the survey questions, the data are not representative of independent living programs throughout the country. Data from the 1990 census show, however, that the states responding to the independent living coordinators' survey have 27 percent of the children under age 18 in the United States and represent seven of the 10 U.S. Department of Health and Human Services regions.

Figure 3 shows the distribution of states that responded to the independent living coordinators' survey. In addition, Massachusetts, New York, and Ohio provided information but did not respond to the survey questions.

The Independent Living Program was designed to serve youths who had been in foster care but were not runaways. As noted earlier, however, there

Figure 3. States that responded to NASW's survey of independent living coordinators. (Shaded states responded.)

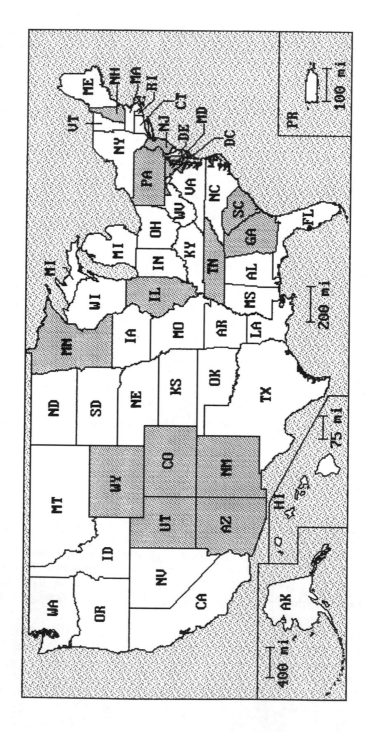

appears to be considerable overlap in the two populations. Some states recognize this overlap. For example, the New York State regulations (New York State Department of Social Services, 1987) state that "a child deemed to have a goal of independent living means a child sixteen years of age or older who *resided in foster care for at least twelve months within the past thirty-six months* and who has a goal of discharge to parents or relatives or a goal of adoption." That same child could have been a runaway before he or she entered care.

The New York State regulations also anticipate that some youths who have been in foster care and in the independent living program will become runaway or homeless. Thus, the regulations require a six-month trial discharge, stating that "in the event that the child becomes homeless during the period of trial discharge, the district must assist the child to obtain housing" (New York State Department of Social Services, 1987). The regulations further state, "After the district's custody of the child has terminated whether by court order or by the district's own action, the district must maintain supervision of the child until the child is twenty-one years of age, where the child has been discharged to independent living or is learned to have been discharged to independent living and has permanently left the home of his or her parents or relatives prior to the termination of the district's custody."

As would be expected in similar populations, youths in the Independent Living Program face many problems similar to those faced by runaway and homeless youths. The state independent living coordinators were not asked to give percentages of youths who had different types of problems, but they were asked to identify the types of problems that have changed significantly over the last five years for the youths in their programs. From the most frequently mentioned problems (identified in Table 12), it is clear that youths in the foster care independent living program (in the states that

Table 12. Problems of Youths in Foster Care Independent Living Programs

Problem	Number of Respondents ($n = 10$)[a]
More homeless families	9
More sexual abuse by parent or caretaker	8
More parental drug abuse	8
More parental alcoholism	7
More mental health problems among youth	7

[a] Ten out of 14 states responding answered this question.
Source: NASW, 1991 Survey of State Independent Living Coordinators.

responded) have many of the same problems faced by runaway and home-less youths in shelters.

A comparison of the survey respondents' primary services—those offered by the providers who responded to the questionnaire on runaway and homeless youth compared with services provided by the state independent living pro-grams—show a few significant differences (Table 13). Far more (100 percent) of the independent living programs provide a program for alcoholics than do the programs for runaway and homeless youths (18 percent). This is surprising

Table 13. Comparison of Services Offered by Shelters and Independent Living Programs (ILPs)

Service	Percentage of Shelters	Percentage of State ILPs
Screening/intake	96	100
Refer to program for alcoholics	86	100
Provide program for alcoholics	18	100
Refer for mental health services	90	100
Help youth develop independent living plan	70	100
Provide independent living skills training	63	100
Refer to educational program/GED	82	100
Information and referral	98	93
Provide individual counseling	98	93
Refer for transportation	45	93
Provide transportation	75	93
Refer for health care	89	93
Refer for other living arrangements	82	93
Provide aftercare services	76	93
Refer to drug abuse program	94	93
Refer for treatment for suicidal behavior	89	93
Refer for employment assistance	71	93
Provide recreation/leisure activities	87	93
Temporary shelter	95	71
Case management	94	86
Provide meals	93	57
Coordinate with juvenile justice system	93	79
Provide family counseling	92	64
Outreach	89	86
Provide advocacy for client	87	86
Refer for family counseling	81	79
Refer for individual counseling	79	86
Provide AIDS/HIV education	79	71

SOURCE: NASW, 1991 Runaway and Homeless Youth Survey and Independent Living Programs Survey.

because a significant number of the programs for runaway and homeless youths have received special drug abuse prevention grants. As expected, far more of the independent living programs also help youths develop independent living plans (100 percent versus 70 percent), provide training in independent living skills (100 percent versus 63 percent), and refer youths for employment assistance (93 percent versus 71 percent).

Very few of the aftercare services provided by these two types of programs are similar. Both provide case management and mental health services, but the aftercare programs for runaway and homeless youths focus on counseling for the individual, family, and parent; group counseling; and counseling for substance abuse problems. Independent living aftercare programs focus more on "hard" services such as education, job training, employment, health care, and financial assistance.

These differences between the independent living programs and the basic center and transitional living programs may not, however, result in significant differences for the youths who receive help from them. The destinations of youths in independent living programs are remarkably similar to those of runaway and homeless youths who are ready for independent living, although fewer independent living program clients than transitional living clients return to the streets.

PROFILE OF HOW PROGRAMS FOR RUNAWAY AND HOMELESS YOUTHS MEET YOUTHS' NEEDS

A program's ability to meet the needs of its youth clients depends on the adequacy of referral sources; on staff members' abilities to draw young people into the programs, assess their problems, and encourage their continued participation; and on the availability of societal and environmental resources to meet the youths' needs.

The primary sources that refer runaway and homeless youths to shelter and transitional living programs are shown in Table 14. Three of the primary referral sources are systems with which youths experience problems. A fourth, public social services, primarily represents the child welfare system (protective services and foster care). Thus, systems designed to respond to long-term needs or to prevent the exacerbation of existing problems are referring youths to short-term shelter programs. The reasons for such referrals are unclear. The referring system's involvement after the referral is made is unknown.

Besides receiving clients through referrals, most shelters conduct activities to increase public awareness so that their programs will receive more referrals. Most shelter providers also offer outreach services to encourage

Table 14. Referral Sources for Shelter and Transitional Living Programs

Referral Source	Percentage of Referrals from Source
Schools	92
Juvenile justice system	91
Law enforcement	91
Public social services	90
Hotline	89

SOURCE: NASW, 1991 Runaway and Homeless Youth Survey.

youths to enter their program. Most outreach is done in schools or through school counselors or special sessions for the students, although a significant number (28 percent) of programs also send street workers out to locations where youths congregate.

When a youth enters a program, almost all providers begin by assessing the young person's needs. Appendix D in this monograph contains two examples of instruments used by providers who responded to the NASW survey. The first instrument is used by The Front Door in Columbia, Missouri, to obtain basic information about the youth and to record any conspicuous behavior or thought-disorder problems. The second instrument is used by the Waterbury Youth Service System of Waterbury, Connecticut. That instrument seems to combine intake and assessment. The staff person using the instrument obtains basic information about the client, records any noticeable personal and mental health problems, and identifies risk factors for substance abuse. This integrated intake and assessment instrument may help providers of short-term services understand the youth's problems more quickly.

Most providers try to identify special problems and needs. Table 15 shows the types of assessments that providers conduct. These assessments

Table 15. Types of Assessments Conducted by Providers

Type of Assessment	Percentage of Programs Conducting
Drug abuse	96
Alcohol abuse	96
Identify mental health problems	91
Identify suicidal ideation	91
Availability of help from nearby relatives	85
Identify health problems (including HIV)	81

SOURCE: NASW, 1991 Runaway and Homeless Youth Survey.

help providers decide what types of services to give the youths. Typical services do not vary much whether or not the provider received a Transitional Living Grant. This is not surprising because most of the providers who received grants also operate shelter programs. Table 16 identifies the services most often offered to youths by 90 percent or more of the providers.

All of the percentages in Table 16 are similar, except that fewer of the transitional living providers coordinated with the juvenile justice system. Although a high percentage do work with the juvenile justice system, it is possible that a more stable living environment and state laws that permit youths to live in transitional facilities help to eliminate status offenses. Besides these services, 90 percent or more of the providers who received Transitional Living Grants offered four additional services, which are listed in Table 17.

Most providers of basic shelter services also offered the services shown in Table 17 except for recreational services. It appears that providers believe that recreational services are essential during longer-term programs or in a residential setting.

As noted earlier in this chapter, the long-term nature of the problems facing runaway and homeless youths means that providers must offer services for extended periods beyond the time that a youth resides in a shelter. Most of the aftercare services are various types of counseling to help youths and their families deal with serious problems. Family counseling, parent

Table 16. Services Most Frequently Offered by Providers

Service	Percentage of All Providers Offering Service	Percentage of Transitional Living Providers Offering Service
Screening/intake	96	96
Temporary shelter	95	91
Information and referral	98	96
Individual counseling	98	96
Case management	94	87
Refer to drug program	94	91
Provide meals	96	96
Family counseling	92	87
Coordinate with juvenile justice	93	83
Outreach	89	96
Refer for mental health services	90	91

Source: NASW, 1991 Runaway and Homeless Youth Survey.

Table 17. Additional Services Offered by Providers

Service	Percentage of All Providers Offering Service	Percentage of Transitional Living Providers Offering Service
Refer for health care	89	91
Refer to program for alcoholics	86	91
Refer for treatment for suicidal behavior	89	91
Provide recreational program	36	96

SOURCE: NASW, 1991 Runaway and Homeless Youth Survey.

and group counseling, and case management can be used to help families deal with communication problems or abuse. These services also can help them access needed services. Case management, individual counseling, and counseling for drug or alcohol abuse may help youths obtain treatment to overcome substance abuse and resolve their problems with the justice system. Parental counseling may encourage parents to seek help for their own substance abuse problems.

Aftercare services may help youths and their families resolve serious problems. These services do not, however, help them deal with some of the most common problems—educational/school problems and long-term economic problems, which prevent a family from achieving self-sufficiency. The stress that these problems cause increases the risk of poor communication or even abuse. Keys to a youth's being able to live independently are completion of high school, or a GED, and a job. These ingredients help him or her attain an adequate income level, which in turn lets the youth pay for decent housing.

Most providers of basic shelter and transitional living services refer youths to programs that will help them get a GED. Only one-third provide an educational program leading to a GED. Most providers also refer youths for employment assistance, because a two-week program simply cannot meet these needs in addition to others.

More providers with transitional living programs offer an educational program/GED (48 percent) and employment assistance (43 percent). These services should become an integral part of the Transitional Living Program because its goal is to help youths become self-sufficient.

To summarize, an early assessment of the Drug Abuse Education and Prevention Program and the Transitional Living Program suggest that they have helped bring about an increased availability of the following services.

- Drug abuse program
- Programs for alcoholics
- Transitional living services
- Independent living skills training
- Aftercare
- GED/educational program
- Employment assistance

The availability of long-term services is essential to meeting the needs of runaway and homeless youths, but the services themselves are not enough. Staff knowledge and skill have a significant impact on a youth's willingness to participate actively in a program.

The staffing of shelters and Transitional Living programs reflects the providers' understanding of the serious long-term problems facing youths who seek their help. Clearly, providers believe that they must have some professionally trained staff in their programs. The percentages of providers using professional staff are shown in Table 18.

The profile of programs for runaway and homeless youths presented in this chapter shows that providers have implemented many new services and programs. An evaluation of the long-term success of their efforts is needed.

Table 18. Professional Staff Employed by Providers Responding to Survey

Profession	Percentage of Providers Employing	Average Percentage of All Employed Staff
BA in social work	74	17
BA in psychology	66	18
BA in counseling	36	9
MSW	61	12
MA in psychology	39	7
MA in counseling	54	11

SOURCE: NASW, 1991 Runaway and Homeless Youth Survey.

References

Finkelhor, D., Hotaling, G., & Sedlak, A. (May 1990). Runaways. In *Missing, abducted, and throwaway children in America: Numbers and characteristics.* (NCJ No. 123667, pp. 171–225). Washington, DC: U.S. Department of Justice, Office of Juvenile Justice and Delinquency Prevention.

Juvenile Justice and Delinquency Prevention Act of 1974 and Related Provisions of Law as Amended through December 31, 1989. Washington, DC: Subcommittee on Human Resources of the Committee on Education and Labor, U.S. House of Representatives.

State Department of Social Services. (1987). *Notice of adoption.* Albany, NY: Author.

Straus, M. (1990). *Abuse and victimization across the life span.* Baltimore: Johns Hopkins University Press.

U.S. Department of Health and Human Services, Administration on Children, Youth, and Families. (1989). *Report to the Congress on independent living initiatives: Fiscal years 1987 and 1988.* Washington, DC: Author.

Program Activities to Meet Youths' Needs

Some providers that participated in the 1991 NASW survey have developed a comprehensive continuum of care for their youth clients. Others have developed a variety of approaches to overcoming problems such as substance abuse. This chapter discusses a range of program activities designed to meet the changing needs of youths.

FULL CONTINUUM OF SERVICES

Some providers that serve youths have developed a full continuum of services or programs, from crisis intervention aimed at family reunification through services to help the young persons adjust to independent living. Dale House, in Colorado Springs, Colorado, is such a facility.

Youths entering Dale House often are referred by other organizations. Other youths entering the facility are former residents or friends of residents. The Colorado Department of Social Services requires that a parent or legal guardian be notified within 24 hours or on the next working day after a youth under the age of 18 enters the facility. If no contact with the parent or guardian can be made, a staff member contacts the Department of Social Services in the youth's county of residence. If a youth refuses to provide personal and eligibility-related information, Dale House staff contact the Youth and Victims Services Division of the Colorado Springs Police Department or the El Paso County Department of Social Services. A staff member contacts the police to determine whether the individual has any outstanding warrants or poses any threat.

At Dale House, crisis telephone, walk-in, and shelter services are available 24 hours a day. Family reunification is the initial goal of these and other services such as providing information and referral, individual counseling, and group counseling. The shelter for youths who are homeless or in crisis is licensed as a Residential Child Care Facility by the state of Colorado.

Dale House continuously conducts outreach to encourage runaway and homeless youths to use the program. The facility's telephone number is given in its media and public service announcements. The National Runaway Switchboard refers youths to Dale House. Staff members regularly speak at local schools to make teachers and students aware of the services Dale House offers, and they also speak at service clubs and churches and appear on radio and television programs.

When family reunification is not possible, Dale House offers an emancipation program leading to legal living independent of parents or guardians in transitional living apartments. Individuals remain in these supervised apartments for four to five months. During this time, they are expected to attain a high school diploma, General Equivalency Diploma (GED), or some form of a vocational education. Clients in the transitional living apartments must participate in "community" groups in which they provide peer support and consultation to each other. Dale House also offers family counseling to encourage improved communication between parent and youth *even when the desirable goal is not family reunification.*

Residents preparing for emancipation attend a weekly emancipation group run by the El Paso County Department of Social Services. Group meetings cover topics such as nutrition, food preparation, health care, sexuality, income tax preparation, and employment skills. Residents have the opportunity to practice some of the skills they learn while living in the supervised apartments by preparing monthly budgets for food, rent, clothing, and other needs. They also plan nutritious meals, cook, and clean house. Staff members help them obtain a social security card, birth certificate, and state identification.

Dale House staff members help youths seek employment. The staff members work with private businesses, Job Training Partnership Act (JTPA) programs, summer job programs, and the Rise Alive Program to obtain employment experiences for residents. When paid employment is not available, staff encourage youths to participate in volunteer work experiences.

Dale House residents participate in developing their own Transitional Living plans. Each resident signs a contract to work on agreed-upon goals. Contracts may cover personal relationships, drug and alcohol abuse, pregnancy, education, employment, savings, health and hygiene, therapy, restitution payments, emancipation skills, and the projected date of discharge.

Upon leaving the apartments, Dale House residents are encouraged to maintain a relationship with the program. Former residents may return for help in obtaining services during crisis situations. When discharged, the residents may obtain silverware, dishes, and cookware from the facility's stockroom, which is stocked through private donations.

COMPREHENSIVE TRAINING FOR SHELTER STAFF

Some programs have comprehensive curricula on prevention, intervention, and treatment for runaway and homeless youths that include information on substance abuse. COMITIS Crisis Center has such curricula.

The COMITIS program consists of two 24-hour help lines that are always staffed by paid personnel. Anyone may go to COMITIS 24 hours a day, for any problem, because it is a crisis center. COMITIS has 20 beds for emergency situations, including 12 beds for troubled youths. It is also licensed by the State Department of Social Services as a Residential Child Care Facility for youths ages three through 17.

COMITIS has a substance abuse program called Drug and Alcohol Time Out, which is a six-week residential program. During the first week, staff members conduct an individual and family evaluation and discuss the benefits of the program. The second week includes drug and alcohol education for the youth and parents. The third week includes individual, parent, and family counseling sessions. During the final three weeks, there are additional individual and family sessions and structured home visits.

The COMITIS training manual includes information on program policies and procedures; procedural information on how to help clients access needed resources; substantive information on the self-help model, communication, and working with clients; substantive information on assessment, treatment, and/or making referrals on child abuse, substance abuse, and potential suicide attempts.

The choice of a general training package to cover most topics or of in-depth specialized training packages probably depends on the type of clients that seek services and on how long the program can offer services. Shelters that have a high percentage of clients with long-term problems may need more specialized training materials on those problems. Shelters and transitional living programs that offer aftercare for substance abuse problems also are more likely to need specialized training materials.

CREATIVE AFTERCARE

Since many youths need long-term assistance to overcome serious problems, aftercare services are extremely important. Even in extended programs, Raychaba (1988) noted that if youths are suddenly cut off from program "family" and friends, they might not be able to overcome their problems.

An innovative aftercare program in Charleston, West Virginia, called Patchwork, has three primary components, which, as discussed below, not only offer additional services but also a continuing support system.

1. BUDDY Program. This component of Patchwork matches a youth of any age with an adult volunteer friend and role model. The program includes light case management, weekly get-togethers for the adult and youth, monthly activities for all program participants, and support from a program coordinator.
2. Aftercare Counseling. This component includes intensive individual or family counseling or both; case management; response and support in crisis situations; and advocacy for obtaining needed educational, legal, or social services. This program includes in-home counseling if the aftercare counselor believes that it is necessary. Parents may attend weekly parent support groups.
3. Good Choices Program. This component includes a 10-week course that meets weekly at the YMCA. During the two-hour sessions, one hour is spent on recreation; the other on teaching concepts of Control Theory. This program is for youths who abuse drugs or alcohol, are in crisis, or are at risk because of a chemically dependent family member. The staff members provide transportation to and from the youths' homes and the YMCA. The recreational counselor helps each youth choose an individualized recreational or creative activity. The youth can choose from any recreational or creative classes that are offered in the community. The recreation counselor helps the youth schedule the activity, however, and provides transportation to and from it. The program pays the fee for the classes. After the course, the youths may choose to meet once a month for a recreational and social get-together. Staff members still provide transportation.

TRANSITION TO INDEPENDENT LIVING

Aftercare services do not sufficiently prepare older homeless youths, or youths for whom independent living is the desirable plan, to take on new roles. Aftercare usually includes services to overcome specific problems or to provide ongoing support.

Transition House is an example of an intensive program designed to prepare homeless youths for independent living. This program emphasizes the development of specific independent living skills, self-esteem, responsibility, and interdependence. Youths have opportunities for experiential learning and for gradually assuming increased responsibility for their own decisions and actions. Participants must work toward the completion of a high school diploma or a GED and must also obtain and keep a part-time job.

Youths enter the Transition House program by moving into a group home. Their first month is spent in orientation and assessment. During this period, staff members assess the youths' strengths and needs and help them establish goals. Group-home residents move through two "learning levels" as they meet individual and program goals. The youths first try to achieve specific individual and program goals. Once residents achieve these goals, staff members help them establish goals for independent decision making and group functioning. When residents show mastery of basic independent living skills and assume responsibility for their behavior, they move to one of two apartments located in the same building as the group home. In the apartments, each of which can house four people, residents can practice independent living in a setting where 24-hour-a-day support and crisis intervention are still available. Apartment residents are also expected to act as advisers and mentors for group-home residents.

The Transition House program also provides follow-up services as youths move into community apartments that a follow-up counselor helps them find. Weekly individual and group counseling as well as crisis intervention and case management are available for a year after a youth leaves the program's building.

TRAINING IN INDEPENDENT LIVING

Independent living programs began before Congress passed the Transitional Living Program. Therefore, the most well-developed approaches in independent-living-skills training for service providers, foster parents, and adolescents come from the independent living programs. (Some shelter and transitional living programs, such as Dale House, do have a strong program component devoted to independent living skills, however.) Two independent living programs are described below.

The Massachusetts Program

The Massachusetts Department of Social Services developed a structured program that involves training social workers and foster parents to help adolescents learn the skills necessary for making the transition to independent living. Foster parents who complete the training for the program, Preparing

Adolescents for Young Adulthood (PAYA), may be reimbursed for the hours of the independent living preparation services they deliver (up to seven hours per week). The PAYA program components include the following:

- *Independent Living Skills Modules.* Module 1 covers home, food, and money management skills. Module 2 provides training on personal care, health, safety, and teen violence. Module 3 addresses education and job skills. Module 4 deals with housing, decision making, transportation, and community resources. Within each module, the foster parent or social worker first conducts an assessment to measure the adolescent's current level of skill mastery. The foster parent, social worker, and youth develop an action plan to build skills in areas that need increased mastery, and the youth then receives exercises and information resources to help as he or she practices independent living skills.
- *PAYA Program Enhancement.* Through interviews and discussion with adolescents participating in the PAYA program and with the foster parent and agency staff, the development of Module 5 targeting teen parents was completed. This Young Parents Module is composed of eight skill-based sections that present resource material and exercises addressing such topics as human reproduction, safe sex, signs of pregnancy, nutrition, child care and development, decision making, and so on. The format for this newer module is similar to the original curriculum (Modules 1 through 4) in having three separate sections: the assessment, the skill plan, and the activity workbook. Although it was designed for pregnant and parenting teens, it is appropriate for use by all adolescents, including females who are not pregnant and males.
- *Incentives.* After completing each PAYA module, a youth may request two incentive awards from the following list: quarterly clothing checks issued in his or her own name; payment for driver's education classes; $100 for deposit in a savings account; $100 for deposit in a checking account; payment of travel expenses (limit $200) to visit a school or college, job site, or training program (this incentive may be used twice); passes to or payment of tuition to a fitness program, museums, and so on; or a $200 savings bond.
- *Lifebook.* Foster parents and social workers help each youth assemble medical, educational, legal, and personal information (for example, medical passport, diploma, GED certificate, birth certificate, social security card, personal photographs) for successful transition to independent living.
- *Videotapes.* "Moving On—Part I" introduces the need for training in independent living skills and the importance of the youth's readiness to learn and practice these skills. "Moving On—Part II" highlights key PAYA concepts and demonstrates use of the independent living skill modules.

The New Hampshire Program

New Hampshire's "Adventure-Based Independent Living Skills Training" provides training in core areas where skills are essential for self-sufficiency. These areas are education and vocational skills, household management, finances, health and nutrition, employment, transportation, and community resources. The objective of the program is to provide a learning experience through active and cooperative participation and to promote understanding of and familiarity with alternatives. Youths have an opportunity to meet with vocational advisers from colleges and vocational institutes, landlords and real estate brokers, health professionals, employment counselors and business managers, automobile dealers and public transportation managers, lawyers, judges, nutritionists, and recreational directors.

The "adventure" part of the curriculum begins with games to help participants become familiar with one another. The intensity of the games increases to create alliances. Participants learn decision-making strategies without the risk of failure. The 15-week curriculum includes warm-up exercises; games—either cognitive, psychomotor, or both; initiative games; initiative problems; trust activities; a low-ropes course; and a medium-ropes course. This adventure-based training increases participants' self-esteem, self concept, and self-confidence. It also develops trust in oneself and others, decision-making skills, cooperative behaviors, positive peer relationships and support, and team-building strategies.

SPECIAL ACTIVITIES TO COMBAT SUBSTANCE ABUSE

Substance abuse is a special area of concern for agencies that serve youths. As noted in Chapter 1 (see Table 3), 23 percent of the youths who seek shelter are drug abusers and 19 percent are alcoholics. Runaway and homeless youths who use drugs are more vulnerable to contracting AIDS, and the use of any substance makes them more likely to commit juvenile offenses to obtain the money they need to buy these substances.

General Substance Abuse Issues for Programs Serving Runaway and Homeless Youths

As noted in Chapter 2 (see Table 10), service providers most often offer seven services that they consider very important. These services show that providers have a clear pattern of service delivery that they feel is essential to intervention and prevention of substance abuse among runaway and homeless youth. During the screening/intake process, staff must be able to identify existing and potential substance abuse problems. Once high-risk and substance-abusing youths are identified, staff must be able either to provide or to refer them to special drug abuse programs or to programs for alcoholics. Shelter providers then continue to offer or refer the youths and their families for ongoing counseling. Shelter staff provide case management.

Assessing Substance Abuse

Despite the short time youths spend in shelters, many providers have found that they need a specialized instrument to identify substance abusers and those at risk of substance abuse. The usefulness of many of these instruments has not been evaluated; the usefulness of others has been evaluated only in certain settings or with specific groups. For example, an instrument designed to identify children of alcoholics was successful in identifying them.

Existing instruments for use with adolescents share certain characteristics. They are designed to assess (1) whether a youth is at high risk of developing substance abuse problems or (2) how far a youth's substance abuse problem has progressed.

Many of the instruments in the first category focus on the home environment and on parental substance abuse problems. Operation PAR, a substance abuse program serving Pinellas County, Florida, developed such an instrument. (Operation PAR is a comprehensive substance abuse prevention, education, and treatment agency. It provides a full continuum of services to the community, including drug abuse prevention in the schools and the community, outpatient programs, and long-term residential treatment for drug dependent youths and adults.) The program's runaway shelter, Family Resources, Inc., uses a modified version of the Operation PAR instrument to identify youths who should be referred to Operation PAR.

The instrument used by staff of Open-Inn, Inc., an Arizona program, determines how far a youth's substance abuse problem has progressed. The purpose of this type of assessment is to determine what type of treatment program would be most appropriate for the youth. The substance abuse assessment instruments used by Family Resources and Open-Inn are reproduced in Appendix E.

Training Staff to Help Youths with Substance Abuse Problems

To be sure that substance abusers and those at risk of becoming substance abusers are identified and receive needed services, some shelters have developed or use special training materials for staff. Directors of shelters and transitional living programs have found that even professionally trained staff need training on the special problems and needs of runaway and homeless youths, especially in substance abuse prevention and intervention.

Open-Inn has developed an extensive training program on substance abuse (Open Inn, undated). The objectives of the program are for trainees to be able to do the following:

- apply substance abuse prevention and intervention concepts to impact substance-abusing youths and their families
- have a working knowledge of the pharmacology of relevant psychoactive drugs used by youths and their families
- assess the degree of substance abuse problems among homeless and runaway youths
- demonstrate an understanding of the root causes, psychodynamics, family dynamics, and social implications of substance abuse and how they affect youths and their families
- use effective communication skills in working with substance-abusing youths
- demonstrate understanding of the implications of substance abuse for HIV infection
- refer substance-abusing youths and their families to appropriate available community resources.

The curriculum of the Open-Inn program includes both basic training on the problems and needs of runaway and homeless youths and specialized training on substance abuse. Training on the former consists of information on some causes of runaway behavior such as child abuse and domestic violence. It also provides opportunities to discuss how some youths react to these problems by committing juvenile property crimes and becoming substance abusers.

Specialized training on substance abuse encompasses genetic and family factors affecting substance abuse, peer factors, psychological factors, biological factors, and community factors. The training also discusses ways to identify a youth's stage of addiction. It then instructs participants on the differences between prevention, intervention, and treatment programs and the necessary skills associated with each type of program. During this portion of the training, participants do role playing to learn the needed skills.

After each unit of the curriculum, participants complete worksheets to determine whether they achieved the training objectives. When they complete the training, participants are expected to be able to answer the questions listed below.

From *Open-Inn Training:* Questions for Program Participants to Answer

Unit I

1. What are five family crises that can contribute to a youth's decision to run away from home?
2. What are ten risk factors faced by homeless and runaway youths?
3. What are two family factors that contribute to substance abuse in youths?
4. What are two biological factors that contribute to a youth's vulnerability to addiction?
5. What are two community factors that raise a youth's vulnerability to substance abuse?
6. What are ten components of the disease model of addiction?

Unit II

7. What are the three A's of a drug epidemic?
8. What are six factors that distinguish adolescent vulnerability to addiction from adult vulnerability to addiction?
9. What are the four stages of addiction in adolescents?
10. What are the four stages of addiction in adults?
11. What are the three components of the N.I.D.A. philosophy?

Unit III

12. How do you define prevention, intervention, and treatment?
13. What are the eight basic counseling skills needed to conduct an assessment interview?

Unit IV

14. What are the key historic trends in the history of mind altering chemicals that characterize its cyclical nature?
15. What are three factors that determine the effect of any drug?
16. What are the major drug categories and what are two drugs in each category?
17. What is a depressant?
18. What is a stimulant?
19. What is addiction?
20. What is dependence?
21. What is tolerance?
22. What is synergism?
23. What is withdrawal?
24. What is an analog?
25. What is euphoria?
26. What is dysphoria?
27. What is a teratogenic effect?
28. What are five different ways to describe a drug?

29. What are the characteristics of the following drug categories with respect to intoxication, withdrawal, overdose, street names, and modes of administration:
    a) CNS depressants
    b) CNS stimulants
    c) narcotics
    d) inhalants/solvents
    e) psychedelics
    f) PCP

Unit V
30. What are five characteristics of a functional family?
31. What are five characteristics that characterize a dysfunctional family?
32. What are the characteristics of the following roles played by dysfunctional family members?
    a) victim
    b) enabler
    c) hero
    d) lost child
    e) mascot
    f) scapegoat

Unit VI
33. Describe the following treatment modalities
    a) out-patient
    b) in-patient
    c) residential
    d) aftercare
34. What are the steps used in the twelve step recovery program?
35. What are three key elements of a treatment plan?

Unit VII
36. What are five reasons for youth workers to be involved in learning about AIDS education, prevention and treatment?
37. What are three barriers to an AIDS prevention effort in each of these categories - personal, professional, community, and agency?
38. What are two ways to remove each of these barriers?

Unit VIII
39. What are seven risk factors for HIV infection associated with substance abuse?
40. What are six adolescent attitudinal barriers to risk assessment for HIV?
41. What is the "3 Plus" approach?

Unit IX
42. What is one youth oriented substance abuse treatment program in each of the following categories, including contact person and phone number:
    a) prevention
    b) out-patient
    c) in-patient
    d) residential
    e) aftercare
43. What are three local resources for self-help and family support for substance abusing youth?

Once participants complete the initial training, they focus on learning to assess risk for, or the stage of, substance abuse. They learn about the different types of substance youths may use and the symptoms they are likely to exhibit. They receive an assessment instrument, which they learn to administer and score.

Substance Abuse in Residential Care

When New York State recognized a growing substance abuse problem among adolescents in residential care, the New York State Council on Children and Families convened an interagency working group to explore ways to improve treatment, prevention, and aftercare for chemically abusing and at-risk youth.

The working group found that 60 percent of youths screened during intake by the Division for Youth needed chemical abuse treatment. Foster care facilities reported that up to 25 percent of their residents abused drugs and alcohol. The Department of Social Services reported that the parents of three out of every four children placed in foster care abused alcohol or drugs (New York State Council on Children and Families, 1990).

The New York State Council's report included the interagency working group's findings and recommendations (Council on Children and Families, 1990). The recommendations are presented below.

- *Recommendation 1: Chemical dependency treatment programs should be established on the grounds of residential institutions to meet the needs of chemical abusing youths in these facilities.* The report suggested that the residential facility could operate the program or could contract with a community treatment agency.

- *Recommendation 2: An outpatient chemical dependency for youth program should be established as a model for serving chemically dependent adolescents in the community.*
- *Recommendation 3: Better linkages should be developed between the residential care system and community programs for treatment of chemical abuse.*
- *Recommendation 4: Uniform procedures and a standardized assessment tool should be implemented for identifying the chemical abuse problems of children entering and in residential care.*
- *Recommendation 5: New York State should strengthen aftercare services for all chemically dependent youth discharged from residential care.* The interagency working group found that there is an absence of structured independent living programs for chemically dependent youths, recovering youths, and youths at high risk of becoming chemically dependent.
- *Recommendation 6: The state should establish structured independent living programs for chemically dependent youth and youth at high risk of chemical dependency who are leaving residential care programs.*
- *Recommendation 7: The state should assist institutional providers with on-grounds schools in identifying and implementing chemical abuse education curricula and early intervention strategies.* The interagency working group specifically recommended that the state use funds authorized by the federal Omnibus Anti-Drug Abuse Act of 1988.
- *Recommendations 8: The residential care system should strengthen its prevention and early intervention efforts through additional staff training and the establishment of prevention professional positions.*

These recommendations are relevant not only for residential programs but for all programs serving runaway and homeless youths. Subsequent to the issuance of the council's report, New York State enacted legislation establishing 100 percent funding for the cost of Outpatient Chemical Dependency for Youth Programs (net of other revenue sources). The Division of Alcoholism and Alcohol Abuse has begun to draft regulations for the Outpatient Chemical Dependency for Youth Programs and will work with the Department of Social Services and the Council on Children and Families in establishing the Medicaid eligibility for this service. In addition, the New York State Department of Social Services is working with the Division of Substance Abuse Services, Division of Alcoholism and Alcohol Abuse, Division for Youth, Office of Mental Health, State Education Department, Council on Children and Families, and child caring agencies to implement a standardized assessment tool for identifying chemical abusing youth entering residential care. These state human service agencies are also collaborating on a model drug and alcohol abuse prevention curriculum for schools serving youth in residential settings.

SUMMARY

This chapter shows that service providers have been very creative in their efforts to meet the needs of runaway and homeless youths and older youths who are making the transition out of foster care. This information and expertise should be shared with all youth-serving agencies that are struggling with similar problems and issues.

References

New York State Council on Children and Families. (1990, March). *Chemical abuse services for youth in residential care.* Albany: Author.

Open Inn, Inc. (Undated). *Open Inn Training.* Tucson, AZ.

Raychaba, B. (1988). *To be on our own with no direction from home.* Ottawa, Ontario, Canada: Youth in Care Network.

4

A "Model" Approach for Serving Runaway and Homeless Youths

A "model" approach to serving clients is not a single existing program or an ideal program that many providers may not be able to achieve. It should be a composite of best practices that can be expected to function together in a program. NASW used data from its 1991 survey and the knowledge and experience of a panel of experts to develop such a model approach. Described below in more detail, this approach includes the following components:

- Identification of education, health, and social service systems and development of linkages for services
- Development and implementation of outreach activities with target populations
- Development and implementation of public awareness activities
- Empowerment of youths and families in the development, implementation, and evaluation of services
- Development and implementation of initial and ongoing assessment tools and mechanisms to identify clients' needs, problems, resources, and progress
- Development of outcome measures and follow-up of service plan to completion or assessment of clients' achievement at three-, six-, and 12-month intervals
- Advocating for quality, client-centered policies, programs, and services for youths and families
- Development and implementation of coordinated programwide and ongoing staff training programs

The author wishes to acknowledge the substantive contribution of Karl Achenbach, PhD, to this chapter.

Planning a Model Program

Service Linkages

The NASW survey of shelter and transitional living providers reveals that, although providers receive referrals from schools, the schools often are unaware of the youths' substance abuse problems when these problems exist. The survey also shows that providers receive referrals from the child welfare system. Thus, shelters and transitional living providers interact with many services delivery and educational systems. For this reason, the first step in developing or improving a program is to identify the systems and the types of linkages that are needed and to negotiate agreements. This process includes determining how to assess youths' needs, access key personnel, get appropriate referrals, and develop cooperative agreements for joint service responsibilities. The joint service responsibilities should include shared case information, joint case planning, and joint follow-up and use of resources.

Agreements for shared service responsibilities do not, however, necessarily identify the services that will be available to youths. Although the NASW survey identifies services that are available nationwide, not all of them are appropriate for every community. Part of the process of establishing linkages is to identify the collective needs of youths in the local community and the services that should be available. Providers can then determine the needs of individual youth and decide how the systems will jointly meet those needs. The resulting case plan gives the provider an accountability mechanism for assessing success.

Outreach Activities

The NASW survey reveals wide variations in the types of activities that providers use for outreach. Although approaches may vary, outreach must establish informal, one-on-one, direct contact with youths wherever they are. Typical target populations for outreach are street youths, youth clients in other public and private agencies or in schools and community centers, youths in "hot" spots such as malls and fast food places, and minority and immigrant youths.

Public Awareness

The NASW survey shows that some providers use similar activities for purposes of both outreach and increasing public awareness. Public awareness activities, however, must be designed to reach a broader audience—civic groups, religious groups, media, professional organizations, funders, public policy bodies, religious organizations, fraternal and civil rights organizations, advocacy organizations, and community and neighborhood groups.

It is important that those designing and carrying out public awareness activities have good communication, marketing, and community organization skills. These experts can develop a plan for reaching all target audiences through a variety of public awareness activities.

Youth and Family Empowerment

Because of the legislation that authorized grants such as the one NASW received for carrying out its 1991 survey on runaway and homeless youths, one focus of the survey was peer counseling. But peer counseling is not the only way that youths should be involved in the services delivery system. Youths and their families need to participate in the entire services delivery process so that services can respond to their needs and help them overcome their problems. Youths and their families should be involved in cooperative case planning, peer support and educational groups, outreach and public awareness, agency and community policymaking, experiential sharing, and advocacy. Each organization needs to assess how youths currently participate in the services delivery process and develop plans for increasing their participation.

Assessment

Some providers that responded to the NASW survey could not provide copies of protocols that they use for screening, assessment, and case planning. Assessment is critical, however, if providers are to meet youths' needs. Providers should develop, modify, or use a screening/intake tool, an assessment tool, a protocol for the assessment process to assure its quality, a substance abuse protocol developed jointly with the youth shelter and a substance abuse program, and an individual case plan and a contractual agreement with the client.

The Florida Network of Youth & Family Services suggested that providers use three separate processes and tools: (1) an initial screening to determine eligibility and to obtain demographic information, a description of the presenting problem, an initial risk assessment for suicide and harm to others, and information on the referral source; (2) an intake process to inform the youth and his or her family about the agency and its services and to assess the appropriateness of the services for them; and (3) a more detailed assessment of the client's problems and needs.

Outcome Measures

The NASW survey clearly shows that aftercare is an important and growing part of the services for runaway and homeless youths and their families. It is important to continue to assess clients' progress toward achieving and maintaining the goals of case plans and to refine the plans as necessary while youths are receiving aftercare services. Services and programs employed while youths are in shelters or transitional living programs and those provided after they leave should be evaluated based on individual client outcome and revised as necessary.

Assessment of the client's progress and outcome requires careful documentation of the client's contacts with service providers. It also requires objective assessment of services received and measures of client progress.

Advocacy

The provider's ability to serve youths depends on the availability of services. Therefore, the provider has a responsibility to develop an advocacy plan for developing and maintaining needed services in the community. The provider also should be responsible for documenting the agency's policies and activities.

Staff Training

Many providers responding to the NASW survey did not have a curriculum or materials for their staff training programs, although some used outside experts who might have had these materials. Training for new staff and volunteers is very important, as is training on emerging trends such as substance abuse. The Florida Network of Youth & Family Services recommended that either prior to or immediately after beginning to work for an agency, staff members receive training in first aid, cardiopulmonary resuscitation (CPR), and aggression-control methods. The Florida Network also recommended that all staff who provide counseling services to clients have at least 40 hours of continuing education each year in assessment, treatment methods for individuals, group counseling techniques and procedures, and family counseling therapy and clinical methods.

DEMONSTRATING A MODEL PROGRAM

The Juvenile Welfare Board (JWB) of Pinellas County, Florida, agreed to demonstrate the model approach to service delivery. NASW chose to work with JWB for several reasons.

- JWB is a unique, separate, independent special district of local government with the authority to levy its own taxes for children's services. It is thus in a position to provide future funding in areas of need where certain services or practices have been found to effectively meet that need.
- Key community leaders already participate in the development of policies that govern the distribution of funds for specific services. The JWB Governing Board includes the juvenile court judge, the county superintendent of schools, and the vice chair of the county commission as ex officio members. The governor appoints five additional community members to four-year terms. This board votes the tax levy, establishes policy, adopts the annual budget, provides oversight, and employs the JWB executive director. This allows the establishment of local priorities in response to needs that the community identifies (Mills, 1985).
- JWB had already participated in a countywide needs assessment process and could readily identify some areas of need.

The Juvenile Welfare Board obtained an agreement with an operator of two runaway shelters, Family Resources, Inc., of St. Petersburg, Florida, to participate in the demonstration. After the model approach had been developed, JWB and Family Resources began to assess the state of services for runaway and homeless youths in Pinellas County. By comparing local data with national data acquired through the NASW survey, JWB and Family Resources were able to identify gaps. The gap most important to the demonstration was the underrepresentation of minorities in programs for runaways. They then chose to focus on parts of the model approach described above. The key components of each part of the model approach are repeated below, with a description of how Pinellas County chose to address or document existing activities that support each element.

Service Linkages—Demonstration Program

Model Component: Linking services includes determining how to assess youths' needs, access key personnel, get appropriate referrals, and develop cooperative agreements for joint service responsibilities. The joint service responsibilities should include shared case information, joint case planning, and joint follow-up and use of resources.

Pinellas County Activities. The Juvenile Welfare Board conducted a county-wide human services needs assessment in cooperation with the Interagency Committee on Planning and Evaluation (I-COPE). I-COPE was established as a voluntary organization of public and voluntary planning and funding agencies to improve the quality and coordination of planning, funding, and evaluation activities among Pinellas County human services providers. The first community needs assessment resulted in a detailed plan for Pinellas County to follow. Adolescent substance abuse became a first-level priority for the use of resources. The needs assessment has served as a major basis for guiding JWB's research, planning, training, advocacy, and allocation decision for the past five years (Juvenile Welfare Board of Pinellas County, 1988).

I-COPE is currently conducting a second community needs assessment. Its primary purposes are to assess progress made in meeting the previously identified needs, to identify new and emerging needs, and to develop a community plan for addressing the needs over the next five years.

In addition to using information from the needs assessment, Family Resources participated in NASW's nationwide survey. While gathering data for the survey, Family Resources management became more aware that the local minority population was underserved by its runaway program. Table 19 shows that Family Resources had served very few nonwhites, particularly males, in the months for which the data were gathered.

Based on the data in Table 19, Family Resources decided to focus the demonstration on outreach to minorities who are or who are at risk of becoming runaway or homeless.

As a result of the Pinellas County needs assessment, Family Resources was already aware that many of the youths that it serves need substance

---

Table 19. Distribution of Sheltered Youths by Race and Gender: October 1, 1990–March 31, 1991

Race	Male	Female	Total
White	130 (30.4%)	209 (48.8%)	339 (79.2%)
Nonwhite	27 (6.3%)	62 (14.5%)	89 (20.8%)
Total	157 (36.7%)	271 (63.3%)	428 (100%)

SOURCE: Achenbach (1992).

abuse services. Additionally, the Florida Department of Health and Rehabilitative Services (HRS) regularly projects the need for substance abuse services. Also, three drug use surveys conducted in 1980, 1984, and 1990 (Juvenile Welfare Board of Pinellas County, Operation PAR, Inc., and the Pinellas County School Board, 1990) revealed that alcohol remains the most highly abused drug in the county; inhalants remain a serious problem; LSD use appears to be increasing; and the use of cocaine, heroin, and marijuana has decreased but is still high. Thus, Family Resources also decided that the demonstration would provide substance abuse prevention and referrals for youths brought into services through the outreach program.

Pinellas County had been and has continued developing many agreements and mechanisms for the coordination of services for runaway and homeless youths. HRS, JWB, and United Way require coordination among agencies that serve the same population or provide similar services. Table 20 lists the agencies with which Family Resources has agreements. Appendix F contains sample copies of some of these agreements.

One of the recently amended agreements that is an essential component of the Pinellas County project is with Operation PAR, a local substance abuse program. Through the amended agreement, Operation PAR gives

Table 20. Index of Family Resources, Inc., Referral Agreements

Agency Name	Date Signed
Sixth Judicial Circuit Court's Psychological Services Unit	1/30/91
All Children's Hospital (ongoing)	4/14/83
Citizens Dispute Settlement Program	1/30/91
Clearwater Police Department Juvenile Division	Ongoing
Florida State Department of Health and Rehabilitative Services	2/14/91
Directions for Mental Health, Inc.	2/06/91
Family Service Centers	3/07/91
Gulf Coast Jewish Family Services, Inc.	1/31/91
Marriage and Family Counseling of Pinellas, Inc.	1/30/91
Pinellas County Sheriff's Department	6/06/91
Professional Comprehensive Addiction Services	1/18/91
Mental Health Association, Inc.	2/11/91
Suncoast Child Protection Team	Ongoing
Suncoast Center for Community Mental Health, Inc.	4/18/91
YWCA Project Help Program	1/31/91
Operation PAR, Inc.	Ongoing

SOURCE: Achenbach (1992).

priority to clients referred by Family Resources. (Previously those clients had been placed on a waiting list.) Operation PAR will provide substance abuse assessments and appropriate referrals as soon as possible. It will also provide survival courses for parents and early intervention school and adolescent interest groups. Operation PAR staff will assess Family Resources staff training needs, develop a training plan, and provide training for Family Resources staff on adolescent substance abuse issues and assessments. In addition, Operation PAR will provide on-site clinical consultation on alcohol and drug screening by Family Resource staff and will attend Family Resource case consultations to provide input on substance abuse issues when appropriate.

An area of particular concern in Pinellas County, based on NASW survey results, was the type of agreements governing the relation between public foster care services and the programs for runaway and homeless youths.

Family Resources has a contract with HRS to provide residential and non-residential services to Children in Need of Services and Families in Need of Services (CIN/FINS). These are preventive services for children who are at risk of running away or who have already run away or who are beyond parental control, are truants, or have school problems. To maintain the integrity of the shelter program, Family Resources will not accept an emergency shelter contract with HRS for children who require ongoing services.

Family Resources' runaway shelters are licensed for a total of 20 beds, but only 18 are funded, leaving two for emergencies or overflow. Youths referred by HRS are reviewed on a case-by-case basis, with a clear understanding that shelter stay is for a maximum of 48 hours. Overall, cooperation from HRS counselors and supervisors is good. They understand that if there are problems related to emergency shelter placements, Family Resources will stop taking them. As infrequently as HRS does refer youths, the referrals are typically situations of critical need, and HRS strictly adheres to the 48-hour maximum.

Outreach—Demonstration Program

Model Component: Outreach must establish informal, one-on-one, direct contact with youths wherever they are. Typical targets for outreach are street youths, youth clients in other public and private agencies or in schools and community centers, youths in "hot" spots such as malls and fast food places, and minority and immigrant youths.

Pinellas County Activities. Family Resources staff felt that they needed to concentrate outreach efforts on minorities, but because minorities—especially males—are not well represented in Family Resources programs, staff members were not sure how to reach runaways or homeless minority youths. Consequently, Family Resources began by conducting outreach activities with all high-risk youths in two neighborhoods.

The neighborhoods were selected because the socioeconomic status of most residents and other indicators make them high-risk neighborhoods for youths. Most of the minority residential areas in Pinellas County where Family Resources operates are in St. Petersburg, in the southern part of the county and in Clearwater in the north. St. Petersburg has a much higher proportion of nonwhite residents than does Clearwater; much of the southern half of the city houses many black people. There are fewer black people in the north, and they tend to live in geographically isolated enclaves rather than in large neighborhoods. The socioeconomic status of black people in the north is higher than that of those in the south.

For this project, Family Resources hired two new minority outreach workers with extensive experience in the community. They began working in August 1991. One outreach worker focused exclusively on St. Petersburg, the other on Clearwater.

Major points of possible contact with youths who are at risk of running away or becoming homeless or who have run away previously in St. Petersburg are five housing projects, a local community center, and local convenience stores (Achenbach, 1992). Major points of contact in Clearwater are a low-income minority neighborhood, a local housing project, a local youth club, and a local neighborhood association.

The outreach workers tried very different approaches (Achenbach, 1992). The worker in the southern part of the county did traditional street work, "hanging out" on the streets and playgrounds of community centers. The worker in the northern part of the county, an established member of the community, worked within an agency setting, establishing relationships with personnel of other agencies in the area. Both outreach workers spent the first three weeks on the job making contacts and developing linkages with community organizations and residents. Actual street work began in early September. Both workers track weekly community contacts and log client contacts. Information from these contacts is being entered into two databases created by Achenbach. (Appendix G contains the outreach worker client contact log, community contact log, and the form used to collect client information.)

The outreach activity also includes a follow-up worker, who is responsible for collecting follow-up information by phone or mail from youths and families served by the demonstration program (Achenbach, 1992). This worker was also responsible for developing the baseline data from the previous year of the shelter program for comparison purposes.

JWB will assess the effectiveness of outreach activities in part by having the follow-up worker interview youths who stopped participating in the outreach program and also interview the youths' families.

Public Awareness—Demonstration Program

Model Component: Public awareness activities should reach civic groups, religious groups, media, professional organizations, funders, public policy bodies, fraternal and civil rights organizations, advocacy organizations, and community and neighborhood groups.

NASW Activities. NASW took responsibility for developing a public service announcement (PSA) that would be useful not only in Pinellas County for the demonstration activities but also throughout the country for increasing public awareness about the needs of runaway and homeless youths.

Of the 150 stations that received the PSA nationwide, 80 percent (119) aired it or plan to include it in future rotations. These stations represent 35 states and the District of Columbia and include cable, affiliates of all three major networks, independent stations, and Spanish-language stations.

Pinellas County Activities. Pinellas County primarily planned to use the public service announcement developed by NASW. The Juvenile Welfare Board received copies of the PSA from NASW in January 1992 and gave them to Family Resources for distribution. The tapes were distributed to four local network affiliates, the public broadcasting station, one independent TV station, and two cable companies. One station, Channel 28 (WFTS-FOX), began airing the announcement on February 14, 1992.

Family Resources is responsible for the Florida Runaway Network Hotline (1-800-RUN-AWAY), and before distributing copies of the PSA, it had this hotline number added. Family Resources planned to monitor any increases in the number of calls received once the PSA had started airing. However, for reasons unknown, the number of calls was already increasing. Calls increased from 63 in November to 95 in December to 128 in January. The increasing number of calls before the PSA was released in Florida could make it difficult to assess its impact.

Youth and Family Empowerment—Demonstration Program

Model Component: Programs should involve youths and their families in cooperative case planning, peer support and educational groups, outreach and public awareness, agency and community policymaking, experiential sharing, and advocacy.

Pinellas County Activities. Because the major emphasis of the demonstration is on outreach, Family Resources planned to empower youths by increasing their participation in outreach activities, in decisions to use services, and in case planning.

Peer counselors are used in various capacities at Family Resources including that of continuing outreach efforts when youths first enter the program. The peer counselors' role in the outreach component of this project is primarily that of educators. Currently, peer educators are working 10 hours per week meeting with youths in the shelters and coleading substance abuse prevention and education groups. The peer educators work with program counselors to provide Abilities Confidence Training (ACT) classes. ACT is a licensed substance abuse prevention education program.

Assessment—Demonstration Program

Model Component: It is important to develop, modify, or use a screening/intake tool, an assessment tool, a protocol for the assessment process to assure its quality, a substance abuse protocol developed jointly with the youth shelter and a substance abuse program, and an individual case plan and contracting agreement with the client.

Pinellas County Activities. Family Resources decided to concentrate on the substance abuse protocol. Staff members received training from Operation PAR in substance abuse assessment and are using a modified version of the protocol established by PAR. The project will document changes in the appropriateness of referrals before and after staff received training in the use of the protocol.

Outcome Measures—Demonstration Program

Model Component: It is important to continue to assess clients' progress toward achieving and maintaining the goals of case plans and to refine the plans as necessary. It is also important to assess the impact of program activities on overall client outcomes.

Pinellas County Activities. Family Resources decided to compare the outcomes of all youths who enter their programs through the new outreach component, which targeted minorities, with the outcomes of youths who have been in the programs previously. This will help staff members determine whether the outreach activity is helping to improve outcomes for minority youths.

A total of 280 youths were enrolled in the program by the two outreach workers—178 in the northern part of the county and 102 in the southern part of the county. The workers used the following three methods to encourage the youths to participate.

Table 21. Family Resources' Mode of Client Contact by Outreach Location in Pinellas County: October 1, 1991–January 31, 1992

Chi-Square = 46.6; $DF = 2$; $p = .0001$

Location	Individual	Group	Presentation	Totals
Northern Pinellas County	28 (15.73%)	48 (26.97%)	102 (57.3%)	178 (100%)
Southern Pinellas County	42 (41.18%)	43 (42.16%)	17 (16.67%)	102 (100%)
Total	70 (25.00%)	91 (32.5%)	119 (42.5%)	280 (100%)

SOURCE: Achenbach (1992).

1. Individual: one-on-one interviews with the youth or individual referral from a teacher or community center
2. Group: informal gatherings of youths at a community center or playground
3. Presentation: a formal presentation or session coordinated by the outreach worker, for example, at a service agency or a church.

Table 21 shows the type of contact made with at-risk youths through the outreach program. Table 22 shows the gender of clients reached at each outreach location. Table 23 shows the race of clients contacted at each outreach location.

Even after just four months the demonstration was clearly reaching the minority population. It also was trying to reach youths for whom a desirable

Table 22. Gender of Clients by Outreach Location in Pinellas County

Chi-Square with continuity correction = 8; $DF = 1$; $p = .0046$

Location	Female	Male	Totals[a]
Northern Pinellas County	105 (59.0%)	73 (41.0%)	178 (100%)
Southern Pinellas County	41 (40.6%)	60 (59.4%)	101 (100%)
Total	146 (52.3%)	133 (47.7%)	279 (100%)

[a] For one youth, gender and race is unknown.
SOURCE: Achenbach (1992).

Table 23. Race of Clients by Outreach Location in Pinellas County

Total Chi-Square = 10.1; *DF* = 4; *p* = .0394

Location	Black	White	Asian	Hispanic	Unknown	Totals
Northern Pinellas County	149 (83.7%)	26 (14.6%)	3 (1.7%)	0 (0%)	0 (0%)	178 (100%)
Southern Pinellas County	94 (92.2%)	6 (5.9%)	0 (0%)	1 (1.0%)	1 (1.0%)	102 (100%)
Total	243 (86.8%)	32 (11.4%)	3 (1.1%)	1 (0.4%)	1 (0.4%)	280 (100%)

SOURCE: Achenbach (1992).

plan would be greater independence. Although there is a continuum of increasing responsibility for youths, the evaluation also looked at the ages of the youths contacted through outreach to assess whether they tended to be older youths. The ages of the youths ranged from seven to 22, with a mean of 12.8 (+/-0.2). Almost 25 percent of the youths contacted in the southern part of the county were 16 or 17 years old. Approximately 17 percent of the youths contacted in the northern part of the county were 16 or 17.

Although the outreach workers contacted 280 at-risk youths, they only referred 43 of the youths for further services. Table 24 shows the agencies to which the 43 youths and their families were referred. Some of the youths or families or both received referrals to more than one agency.

Advocate for Quality, Client-Centered Policies, Programs, and Services for Youths and Families—Demonstration Program

Model Components: The provider's ability to serve youths depends on the availability of services. Therefore, the provider has a responsibility to develop an advocacy plan for developing and maintaining needed services in the community.

Planned Pinellas County Activities. The outreach workers are currently documenting major policy issues and barriers to service delivery. The follow-up worker will examine these same issues as they relate to prior clients. Family Resources will develop a plan for addressing those issues and barriers.

At the time this monograph was written, only seven clients had been in the program long enough to receive a three-month follow-up of their service plan. This information is inadequate to identify any barriers to service or ways in which the program helped clients reach their goals.

Table 24. Agencies Receiving Referrals

	Number of Referrals		
Agency	Southern Pinellas County	Northern Pinellas County	Total
Youth Club	0	8	8
Family Resources School Based	1	6	7
Vocational Rehabilitation	6	1	7
Juvenile Services Program	6	0	6
Family Resources Outclient	1	3	4
Project P.A.I.R.	4	0	4
Urban League	0	4	4
Workforce	2	0	2
Family Service Center	2	1	3
Family Resources Shelter	0	2	2
Operation PAR (substance abuse)	0	3	3
Marriage and Family Counseling	0	2	2
Social Services	0	2	2
Alateen	0	1	1
Girls Club	0	1	1
Door of Hope	1	0	1
Enoch Davis Center	1	0	1
Frank Pierce Center Teen Group	1	0	1
Gulf Coast Legal	1	0	1
Job Corps	0	1	1
Mount Zion Human Service	1	0	1
Oasis	1	0	1
St. Pete Health Clinic	1	0	1
Tough Love	0	1	1
Total number of referrals	29	36	65
Number of clients referred	22	21	43

SOURCE: Achenbach (1992).

Develop and Implement Coordinated Programwide and Ongoing Staff Training Programs—Demonstration Program

Model Component: Training for new staff and volunteers and ongoing training on emerging trends is important.

Planned Pinellas County Activities. Operation PAR, the substance abuse program, trained Family Resources staff in the area of substance abuse. The JWB Training Center is providing other training as needed.

Table 25. Outreach Worker Training

Date	Topic	Training Facility	Northern Pinellas County Worker	Hours	Southern Pinellas County Worker	Hours
9/9/91	Working Effectively with Black Juvenile Delinquents: From the Young Black Male's Perspective	Juvenile Welfare Board (JWB)	Yes	3	Yes	3
10/8/91	Do the Right Thing: Exploding Prevention Myths	JWB, PAR	No		Yes	3
10/11/91	Getting to the Heart of the Matter with Black Males: Critical Intervention Strategies That Work	JWB	Yes	8	Yes	8
10/29/91	Working with Children and Families Impacted by Homelessness	JWB, YWCA, Suncoast CMH	No		Yes	3
10/29/91	Working with Adults and Children with AIDS	JWB	No		Yes	3
11/5/91	Working with Delinquent Youth	JWB, Juvenile Services	Yes	3	No	
1/21/92	AIDS/HIV Training	Family Resources	Yes	4	No	
1/23/82	Self-Esteem	Love, Faith and Hope Development Center	Yes	8	Yes	8
1/28/92	Identifying and Assessing Substance Abuse Problems	PAR	Yes	3	Yes	3

SOURCE: Achenbach (1992).

Training for the two outreach workers began in September 1991. Table 25 shows the training that the outreach workers received.

Although the demonstration described in this chapter is continuing, it is clear that the model approach helped JWB and Family Resources identify minority youths' needs for services and develop an approach to reach them. It may be a useful process for other communities as well.

References

Achenbach, K. (1992). *NASW Demonstration Project year end report: July 1, 1991–February 28, 1992.* Jacksonville: University of South Florida.

Juvenile Welfare Board of Pinellas County. (1988). *Annual analysis of performance data for funded program, fiscal year 1987-88: Executive summary.* St. Petersburg, FL: Author.

Juvenile Welfare Board of Pinellas County, Operation PAR, Inc., and the Pinellas County School Board. (1990, July 24). *Drug use and abuse among students in Pinellas County.* Pinellas County, FL: Author.

Mills, J.E. (1985, November 8). *Dedicated tax levies: an untapped funding resource?* Paper presented at the NASW Professional Symposium. Chicago.

Summary, Issues, and Recommendations

The problems facing vulnerable youths have been well documented both by NASW's 1991 survey and by other studies cited in this monograph. Many of these youths have been abused by parents or have parents who are substance abusers. Most perform poorly in school and have low self-esteem. The widespread availability of drugs has intensified these problems. Once youths run away, they are likely to suffer from poor nutrition, respiratory diseases, physical and sexual victimization, and many other problems.

Agencies that serve young people are trying a variety of innovative prevention, intervention, and treatment approaches to help youths deal with their problems. The relative success of these approaches has yet to be determined because programs such as the Transitional Living Program and the Drug Abuse Education and Prevention Program are relatively new.

As providers struggle to help youths overcome their problems, the nationwide NASW survey and the comparisons with other studies provided in this monograph raise a number of serious issues that should be of concern to policymakers, researchers, and providers. Some of the key issues and possible ways to deal with them are discussed below.

ISSUE 1: MANY YOUTHS ARE NOT RECEIVING SERVICES

Only a fraction of the youths who run away or are homeless seek help from shelter providers. The study conducted for the Office of Juvenile Justice and Delinquency Prevention (U.S. Department of Justice, 1990) showed that few runaways use shelter programs, which makes the need for improved outreach and public education obvious. Outreach probably should be conducted in several ways. First, teachers and school officials should be educated about services that are available for youths. Second, school administrators should receive training in how to support teachers who suspect that a youth is at risk of running away or has run away. (It is difficult for a teacher to address the problem because of the large number of students depending on him or her.) Third, information about alternatives to running away and the services that are available should become part of school curriculum. The Family and Youth Services Bureau (FYSB) of the U.S. Department of Health and Human Services can encourage the development and dissemination of training materials and curricula through research and demonstration projects. FYSB could also work with groups that represent teachers and school administrators to encourage local school districts to use the materials and curriculum. It is up to the local community, however, to assure that these aids are used.

ISSUE 2: ADDRESSING LONG-TERM PROBLEMS AND NEEDS IN SHORT-TERM PROGRAMS

More of the youths seeking help in shelter programs have long-term problems than in previous years, and they continue to need help long after they leave the programs. How can shelters maintain the integrity of their original mission to help youths overcome crises and reunite with their families, but also meet the needs of youths who need long-term help?

Many shelters now provide extensive aftercare services and have added services to meet youths' needs. What is the best way to meet the needs of youths with complex crises without overwhelming those who need short-term help? Does a shelter have to develop two separate "tracks"? Does a shelter have to limit the types of long-term problems with which staff will help youths? Family Resources, Inc., in Pinellas County, Florida, will not accept youths who need long-term foster care. Research is needed to determine what types of policies and procedures most effectively help a shelter maintain the integrity of its programs. The most effective policies and procedures then should become part of accepted peer standards for shelter programs.

ISSUE 3: MEETING LONG-TERM PROBLEMS AND NEEDS THROUGH LONG-TERM PROGRAMS

Should the same providers who offer shelter services also qualify for Transitional Living Grants, or do such grants alter the nature of both programs? If using the same providers alters the nature of the programs, would requiring different providers prevent a provider from developing a full continuum of services for youths? To what extent should a transitional living program include the components of a shelter program rather than just serve as a next step on a continuum of programs available to youths?

To answer some of these questions, research is needed to determine how many youths move from a shelter to a transitional living program, and how many enter the transitional living program directly. The research also should determine whether the youths' services needs when they enter the transitional living program vary by the types of services they received previously.

ISSUE 4: CONTINUING SUPPORT AFTER LEAVING PROGRAMS

Raychaba (1988) indicated that when youths leave foster care, they find themselves immediately without income, housing, a social support system. This is often true for youths leaving shelters or transitional living programs. Even when providers offer aftercare, once youths complete the aftercare program, they have limited contact with staff and former residents of the shelter or transitional living program. (There are some exceptions, such as Dale House, discussed in Chapter 3.)

How should youths' needs for support be met? What additional funding and program activities would be necessary? Additional research with the youths themselves might reveal the types of support that are most needed.

ISSUE 5: FOSTER CARE REFERRALS

A high percentage of runaway and homeless youths were in foster care the year before they ran away or became homeless. Many shelters and transitional living programs receive referrals from child protective services and foster care.

Some professionals have suggested that screening tools designed to identify children and youth who have probably been abused are, in fact, being used to screen out these young persons—particularly in states that are strapped for resources. These professionals believe that such youths end up at a shelter, although there are no data to confirm or deny this. Except in communities like Pinellas County where there is good documentation, the relation among state child protective services, state foster care programs, and programs for runaway and homeless youths is unknown. It can be understood only through an in-depth look at differences between communities where shelters have high proportions of youths who have been in foster care and communities where that proportion is low. Research is needed to examine the current relationship between programs for runaway and homeless youths and foster care in these different communities so that providers can better understand how to structure the relationships to assure that appropriate types of services are available to youths. The research should include an assessment of staff and foster parent/group-home staff training needs.

At least three separate program systems have a stake in this issue in terms of the way youths access and receive services—state protective services, state foster care programs, and programs for runaway and homeless youths. Certain minimum standards or expectations should be established regarding the relationships among these programs. The Family and Youth Services Bureau will soon be developing a peer review system for the runaway and homeless youth programs. State foster care systems are already subject to Section 427 of the Social Securities Act requirements and case reviews. Minimum expectations for at least written agreements could be built into state requirements.

ISSUE 6: RELATIONSHIPS WITH OTHER PROGRAMS SERVING OLDER YOUTHS

Programs for runaway and homeless youths and foster care Title IV-E Independent Living Program are serving youths with similar problems and may be serving some of the same youths at different times.

FYSB is currently funding some projects to help these programs develop collaborative agreements for training staff and serving youths. The results of these projects should be synthesized and widely disseminated. Independent living programs and programs for runaway and homeless youths should be encouraged to develop collaborative agreements. As these agreements are tested, it would be useful for grantees to identify any legislative and administrative barriers to serving youths effectively.

ISSUE 7: STAFFING PROGRAMS FOR RUNAWAY AND HOMELESS YOUTHS

Most shelters and transitional living programs employ professionally trained staff. Most employ social workers. Many employ psychologists or counselors. Providers obviously have decided they need the professionals, because there are no federal requirements for professionally trained staff. Research is needed to determine in what capacities providers prefer different types of staff.

Shelters and transitional living facilities offer an exhaustive array of services. It may be useful to group these services into basic components (for example, outreach, health, education, counseling) and to identify the staffing needs (professional and nonprofessional) of each component.

SUMMARY

Although programs face many other issues and problems as they try to serve youths with serious problems and their families, the issues discussed here were the ones consistently identified through NASW's 1991 survey. They are not impossible issues to resolve. They can be addressed through research, negotiated agreements between programs, or changes of an administrative or policy nature.

Critical to progress in meeting the needs of vulnerable youths is continued research, dissemination of research findings, and the ability of more communities to participate in research and demonstration projects. Although it is necessary for each component of a comprehensive system of care for youths to be researched separately, each community must have a full continuum of care if youths and their families are to overcome problems successfully and lead productive lives.

References

Finkelhor, D., Hotaling, G., & Sedlak, A. (May 1990). Runaways. In *Missing, abducted and throwaway children in America: Numbers and characteristics.* (NCJ No. 123667, pp. 171–225). Washington, DC: U.S. Department of Justice, Office of Juvenile Justice and Delinquency Prevention.

Raychaba, B. (1988). *To be on our own with no direction from home.* Ottawa, Ontario, Canada: National Youth in Care Network.

A · Description of the NASW Survey and Analysis of Findings

DESIGN OF A QUESTIONNAIRE

The National Association of Social Workers (NASW) convened a panel of technical experts to provide advice in the design of a questionnaire. Members of the Technical Advisory Panel are listed below.

Marion F. Avarista
Executive Director
Travelers Aid of Rhode Island

Edward Bradford
Senior Program Analyst
Administration on Children,
   Youth, and Families
Family and Youth Services Bureau

Della M. Hughes
Executive Director
The National Network of Runaway
   and Youth Services, Inc.

Gail L. Kurtz
Executive Director
Southeastern Network of Youth
   and Family Services

James Mills
Executive Director
Juvenile Welfare Board of Pinellas
   County, Florida

Carol Smith
Director
School of Social Work and
   Attendance
School Board of Broward County,
   Florida

The panel recommended that some of the terms used in the questionnaire be defined. The definitions mailed with the questionnaire and a copy of the questionnaire follow this discussion.

TESTING OF THE QUESTIONNAIRE

Questionnaires for runaway and homeless youth shelter providers were sent to 17 sites as a pretest. The sites selected had substance abuse prevention or intervention programs. Ten shelters completed and returned the questionnaire. No respondent had significant problems with the questionnaire; therefore, no modifications were necessary. The pretest responses became part of the database.

THE SURVEY

Between January and April 1991, NASW surveyed 360 agencies, including runaway and homeless youth shelters that receive funding from the Administration on Children, Youth, and Families (ACYF) to provide basic shelter and crisis intervention services and providers that receive funding to provide transitional living services to homeless youths. Many of these services providers also received Drug Abuse Prevention and Education Grants. NASW also surveyed state coordinators of independent living services.

SURVEY RESPONSE

A total of 169 agencies, or 47 percent of the providers surveyed, responded to NASW's survey. The responses include 23 of the 45 providers who received first-year Transitional Living Grants from ACYF. Below is the final breakdown of respondents by the type of ACYF funding they receive.

Type of Funding	Number of Providers
Basic center	100
Basic center and drug prevention	24
Basic center and transitional living	18
Basic center, transitional living, and drug prevention	2
Drug prevention	1
Transitional living	2
Transitional living and drug prevention	1
None or not identified	21

The data are nationally representative, including responses from 44 states and territories in every region of the U.S. Department of Health and Human Services.

Analysis of the Data

To be certain that the data are nationally representative, project staff generally determined what percentage of respondents answered a question, then multiplied the average response by that percentage. This assumes that anyone who did not respond to the question would have entered a zero. Thus, the analysis provides the *minimum* extent of each problem identified or amount of each service provided.

Definitions of Terms in Questionnaire

Note: Many of these definitions are drawn from Barker, R. L. (1987). *The social work dictionary.* Silver Spring, MD: National Association of Social Workers.

Advocacy: actions to represent or defend the client.

Aftercare: services provided beyond the time a youth spends in a shelter or transitional living situation.

Alcohol Abuse: see Substance Abuse

Assessment: the process of determining the nature, cause, progression, and the prognosis of a problem and what can be changed to minimize or resolve it. Assessments for alcohol or drug abuse problems include, for example, identification of risk factors such as parental drug or alcohol abuse and tolerant attitudes toward consumption of such substances.

Case Management: a procedure to coordinate all the helping activities on behalf of a client or a group of clients, including comprehensive multidimensional assessment, periodic reassessment, coordination of services, and monitoring and evaluation of client progress.

Counseling: giving advice, delineating alternatives, helping to articulate goals, and providing needed information.

Drug Abuse: see Substance Abuse

Independent Living Plan: a written plan, based on a needs assessment, to help the participant identify and access needed services and training and develop goals and a strategy for achieving those goals.

Independent Living Skills Training: training in daily living skills, budgeting, locating and maintaining housing, and career or employment related planning (including an educational program leading to a high school diploma, training, and job-related counseling).

Information: a service to inform clients about existing benefits and programs in the community and the procedures for obtaining and using them.

Information and Referral: a service that provides information and helps clients find other appropriate sources of help. It may or may not include follow-up. For this survey, follow-up to referral should be checked separately.

Intake: when a client seeks service, providing information about the conditions of service (e.g., rules), obtaining basic information about the client, arriving at an agreement with the client about willingness to be served by the program.

Intervention: actions taken to solve or prevent problems or achieve goals.

Mental Health Services: clinical preventive and social services provided by psychiatrists, psychologists, psychiatric nurses, and social workers.

Outreach: services designed to inform individuals about the program and attract those who are eligible to participate in the program.

Prevention: actions taken to minimize and eliminate social, psychological, or other conditions (such as alcohol and drug abuse) known to cause or contribute to physical and emotional illness.

Transitional Living: living arrangement with a program to help youth pass from a stage of dependency on adults to independent living.

Substance Abuse: a disorder related to the unhealthy use of alcohol or drugs. To be considered a substance abuser, an individual must have used the substance for over one month; had social, legal, or vocational problems as a result of its use; and developed a pathological pattern of use (episodic binges) or psychological dependence (a desire for continued use and an inability to inhibit that desire).

Questionnaire
SERVICES FOR RUNAWAY AND HOMELESS YOUTH

Name and Title of Person Responding:

Agency:

Telephone Number and State:

Agency and Program Characteristics

We are trying to identify key elements that help you respond to the needs of runaway and homeless youth, including agency characteristics, the services you offer, and the training you give your staff. We especially want to know which elements enhance your ability to intervene or prevent substance abuse among youth.

1. Check any items that describe your services for runaway and homeless youth. Check all that apply.
   1. ___ Emergency shelter
   2. ___ Transitional housing
   3. ___ Housing for emancipated youth
   4. ___ Other (please explain) _____

2. Is your program for runaway and homeless youth in an agency that is—
   1. ___ Private nonprofit
   2. ___ Private for-profit
   3. ___ Public
   4. ___ Other (please specify) _____

3. How many residential facilities for youth do you operate? Please provide actual number. _____

4. How many beds are available in your youth facility/facilities?
   1. ___ Less than 10
   2. ___ 10–14
   3. ___ 15–19
   4. ___ 20
   5. ___ Not applicable

5. Do you use private host homes to provide basic shelter services to youth?
   1. ___ Yes
   2. ___ No (go to question 8)

6. How many host homes do you use? Please provide actual number. _____

7. How many youth stay in a host home each night (estimate average number)?
   _____

8. Which of the following services do you offer to youth? Check all that apply. Please include follow-up to "information and referral" and to any referral under "follow-up to referral."

How important are these services to your ability to intervene/prevent alcohol and drug abuse? Circle answer.

		Very Important	Somewhat Important	Not Very Important
01. ___	Outreach (please specify)	1	2	3
02. ___	Screening/intake	1	2	3
03. ___	Temporary shelter	1	2	3
04. ___	Arrange for meals	1	2	3
05. ___	Provide meals	1	2	3
06. ___	Case management	1	2	3
07. ___	Information and referral	1	2	3
08. ___	Follow-up to referral	1	2	3
09. ___	Refer for individual counseling	1	2	3
10. ___	Provide individual counseling	1	2	3
11. ___	Refer for family counseling	1	2	3
12. ___	Provide family counseling	1	2	3
13. ___	Refer for transportation	1	2	3
14. ___	Provide transportation	1	2	3
15. ___	Refer for health care	1	2	3
16. ___	Provide health care	1	2	3
17. ___	Refer to transitional living beyond shelter	1	2	3
18. ___	Provide transitional living beyond shelter	1	2	3
19. ___	Refer for other living arrangements	1	2	3
20. ___	Organize other living arrangements	1	2	3
21. ___	Refer to aftercare service	1	2	3
22. ___	Provide aftercare services	1	2	3
23. ___	Test for substance abuse	1	2	3
24. ___	Refer to drug abuse program	1	2	3
25. ___	Provide drug abuse program (please attach brief description)	1	2	3
26. ___	Refer to program for alcoholics	1	2	3
27. ___	Provide program for alcoholics (please attach brief description)	1	2	3

Which of the following services do you offer to youth? Check all that apply.

How important are these services to your ability to intervene/prevent alcohol and drug abuse? Circle answer.

	Very Important	Somewhat Important	Not Very Important
28. ___ Provide mental health services	1	2	3
29. ___ Refer for mental health services	1	2	3
30. ___ Provide treatment for suicidal behavior	1	2	3
31. ___ Refer for treatment for suicidal behavior	1	2	3
32. ___ Refer to develop independent living plan	1	2	3
33. ___ Help youth develop independent living plan	1	2	3
34. ___ Provide independent living skills training	1	2	3
35. ___ Refer for independent living skills training	1	2	3
36. ___ Provide recreational program	1	2	3
37. ___ Refer to recreational program	1	2	3
38. ___ Provide educational program/ general equivalency diploma	1	2	3
39. ___ Refer to educational program/general equivalency diploma	1	2	3
40. ___ Provide employment assistance	1	2	3
41. ___ Refer for employment assistance	1	2	3
42. ___ Provide advocacy for clients	1	2	3
43. ___ Refer to agency that will serve as advocate	1	2	3
44. ___ Coordinate with criminal/ juvenile justice system	1	2	3
45. ___ Refer to agency that coordinates with criminal/juvenile justice system	1	2	3
	1	2	3
46. ___ Sponsor peer counseling	1	2	3
47. ___ Refer for peer counseling	1	2	3
48. ___ Provide AIDS/HIV education	1	2	3
49. ___ Refer for AIDS/HIV treatment	1	2	3

Which of the following services do you offer to youth? Check all that apply.

How important are these services to your ability to intervene/prevent alcohol and drug abuse? Circle answer.

	Very Important	Somewhat Important	Not Very Important
50. ___ Provide special services to gay/lesbian youth	1	2	3
51. ___ Refer gay/lesbian youth for special services	1	2	3
52. ___ Provide special services to minority and immigrant youth (with language and cultural barriers)	1	2	3
53. ___ Refer minority/immigrant youth (with language and cultural barriers) to special services	1	2	3
54. ___ Sponsor recreation/leisure time activities	1	2	3
55. ___ Refer for recreation/leisure time activities	1	2	3
56. ___ Other (please specify)	1	2	3

9. Please identify the aftercare services that you provide or to which you refer youth who are transitioning to independent living. Check all that apply.

How important are these services to your ability to intervene/prevent alcohol and drug abuse? Circle answer.

	Very Important	Somewhat Important	Not Very Important
01. ___ Case management	1	2	3
02. ___ Health care	1	2	3
03. ___ Education	1	2	3
04. ___ Job training	1	2	3
05. ___ Employment	1	2	3
06. ___ Counseling for alcoholism	1	2	3
07. ___ Counseling for drug abuse	1	2	3
08. ___ Mental health services	1	2	3
09. ___ Individual counseling	1	2	3
10. ___ Parent counseling	1	2	3
11. ___ Family counseling	1	2	3
12. ___ Group counseling	1	2	3
13. ___ Peer counseling	1	2	3
14. ___ Alternative living	1	2	3
15. ___ Financial assistance	1	2	3
16. ___ Recreation/leisure time activities	1	2	3

Please identify the aftercare services that you provide or to which you refer youth who are transitioning to independent living. Check all that apply.

How important are these services to your ability to intervene/prevent alcohol and drug abuse? Circle answer.

	Very Important	Somewhat Important	Not Very Important
17. ___ None	1	2	3
18. ___ Other (please specify)	1	2	3

_____

10. Are there any youth services you provide today that you did not provide when you first began?

    1. ___ Yes   2. ___ No (go to question 13)

11. Are there any youth services you no longer provide?

    1. ___ Yes   2. ___ No (go to question 13)

12. If you answered yes to question 10 or question 11, please check youth services that changed (please attach explanation). Check all that apply. Please include any follow-up to "information and referral" or to any referral under "follow-up to referral."

	Provide Now but Did Not Initially Provide	No Longer Provide
01. Outreach		
02. Screening/intake		
03. Temporary shelter		
04. Arrange for meals		
05. Provide meals		
06. Case management		
07. Information and referral		
08. Follow-up to referral		
09. Refer for individual counseling		
10. Provide individual counseling		
11. Refer to family counseling		
12. Provide family counseling		
13. Refer for transportation		
14. Provide transportation		
15. Refer for health care		
16. Provide health care		
17. Refer to transitional living beyond shelter		
18. Provide transitional living beyond shelter		
19. Refer for other living arrangements		

	Provide Now but Did Not Initially Provide	**No Longer Provide**
20. Organize other living arrangements	_____	_____
21. Refer to aftercare services	_____	_____
22. Provide aftercare services	_____	_____
23. Test for substance abuse	_____	_____
24. Refer to drug abuse program	_____	_____
25. Provide drug abuse program	_____	_____
26. Refer to program for alcoholics	_____	_____
27. Provide program for alcoholics	_____	_____
28. Provide mental health services	_____	_____
29. Refer for mental health services	_____	_____
30. Provide treatment for suicidal behavior	_____	_____
31. Refer for treatment for suicidal behavior	_____	_____
32. Refer to develop independent living plan	_____	_____
33. Help youth develop independent living plan	_____	_____
34. Provide independent living skills training	_____	_____
35. Refer for independent living skills training	_____	_____
36. Provide recreational program	_____	_____
37. Refer to recreational program	_____	_____
38. Provide educational program/ general equivalency diploma	_____	_____
39. Refer to educational program/ general equivalency diploma	_____	_____
40. Provide employment assistance	_____	_____
41. Refer for employment assistance	_____	_____
42. Provide advocacy for clients	_____	_____
43. Refer to agency that will serve as advocate	_____	_____
44. Coordinate with criminal/ juvenile justice system	_____	_____
45. Refer to agency that coordinates with criminal/juvenile justice system	_____	_____
46. Sponsor peer counseling	_____	_____
47. Refer for peer counseling	_____	_____
48. Provide AIDS/HIV education	_____	_____
49. Refer for AIDS/HIV treatment	_____	_____

	Provide Now but Did Not Initially Provide	No Longer Provide
50. Provide special services to gay/lesbian youth	_____	_____
51. Refer gay/lesbian youth for special services	_____	_____
52. Provide special services to minority and immigrant youth (with language and cultural barriers)	_____	_____
53. Refer minority and immigrant youth (with language and cultural barriers) to special services	_____	_____
54. Sponsor recreation/leisure time activities	_____	_____
55. Refer for recreation/leisure time activities	_____	_____
56. Other (please specify)	_____	_____

_____

_____

Program Staff and Volunteers

We would like to understand how important your staffing is to your ability to intervene/prevent alcohol and drug abuse among youth. Please answer each question and circle how important the response is.

How important are these services to your ability to intervene/prevent alcohol and drug abuse? Circle answer.

	Very Important	Somewhat Important	Not Very Important
	1	2	3

13. What is your staff-to-client ratio in your youth programs? _____   1   2   3

14. What percentage of your staff who serve runaway and homeless youth (full-time and part-time) have a bachelor's degree in—

			Very	Somewhat	Not Very
1. ___	Social work	___%	1	2	3
2. ___	Psychology	___%	1	2	3
3. ___	Nursing	___%	1	2	3
4. ___	Counseling	___%	1	2	3
5. ___	Other (please specify)	___%	1	2	3

_____

15. What percentage of your staff who serve runaway and homeless youth (full-time and part-time) have a master's degree in—

How important are these services to your ability to intervene/prevent alcohol and drug abuse? Circle answer.

			Very Important	Somewhat Important	Not Very Important
1. ___	Social work	___%	1	2	3
2. ___	Psychology	___%	1	2	3
3. ___	Nursing	___%	1	2	3
4. ___	Counseling	___%	1	2	3
5. ___	Other (please specify)	___%	1	2	3

_____

16. What percentage of your program staff serving youth (full-time and part-time) do not have a college degree?___%   1   2   3

17. Do you use volunteers? If yes, how many volunteer hours do you use each month for youth services?   _____hours

18. How do you recruit your staff for youth services? Check all that apply.
    1. ___ Newspaper ads
    2. ___ Word of mouth
    3. ___ Referral from own employees
    4. ___ Referrals from other programs
    5. ___ Former clients
    6. ___ Other (please specify)

_____

19. Do you have a training program for staff serving youth?
    1. ___ Yes
    2. ___ No (go to question 24)

20. If yes, what type of general training is available to the staff serving youth? Check all that apply.

How important are these services to your ability to intervene/prevent alcohol and drug abuse? Circle answer.

		Very Important	Somewhat Important	Not Very Important
1. ___	Orientation (one-half day or less)	1	2	3
2. ___	In-service training (special workshops or continuing education courses of one or more days)	1	2	3
3. ___	Initial work with supervisor	1	2	3
4. ___	None	1	2	3

21. If yes, what type of specialized training is available to your staff? Check all that apply.

How important are these services to your ability to intervene/prevent alcohol and drug abuse? Circle answer.

	Very Important	Somewhat Important	Not Very Important
1. ___ Special training on alcohol and drug abuse	1	2	3
2. ___ Special training on mental health problems	1	2	3
3. ___ Special training on suicidal behavior	1	2	3
4. ___ None	1	2	3
5. ___ Other (please specify)	1	2	3

Clients

We want to understand the roles of various types of agencies that serve different types of clients. The following questions will help us understand the types of youth served by your programs and any special problems they have.

22. What groups of youth do you *primarily* serve?
   1. ___ Youth under 12 years of age
   2. ___ Youth ages 12–14
   3. ___ Youth ages 15–16
   4. ___ Youth ages 17–18

23. What other groups of youth do you serve?
   1. ___ Youth under 12 years of age
   2. ___ Youth ages 12–14
   3. ___ Youth ages 15–16
   4. ___ Youth ages 17–18
   5. ___ Youth over age 18

24. During the past 12 months, what percent of your youth were—
   1. ___ % White
   2. ___ % Black
   3. ___ % Hispanic
   4. ___ % Asian
   5. ___ % Other

25. What were the living situations for homeless/runaway youth who are now ready for transitional living before they came to your organization? Please indicate/estimate the percentage of these youth from each living situation.

How important are these prior living situations to your ability to intervene/prevent alcohol and drug abuse? Circle answer.

			Very Important	Somewhat Important	Not Very Important
01.	Foster home	____%	1	2	3
02.	Parents	____%	1	2	3
03.	Relative	____%	1	2	3
04.	Correctional facility	____%	1	2	3
05.	Group home	____%	1	2	3
06.	Independent living	____%	1	2	3
07.	Runaway or crisis shelter	____%	1	2	3
08.	Friend	____%	1	2	3
09.	On the street	____%	1	2	3
10.	Other (please specify)	____%	1	2	3

_____

26. What percentage of the youth (ready for transitional living) who had/have a substance abuse problem are—
    1. ___ % White
    2. ___ % Black
    3. ___ % Hispanic
    4. ___ % Asian
    5. ___ % Other

27. What percentage of the youth (ready for transitional living) who had/have a substance abuse problem are—
    1. ___ % Male
    2. ___ % Female

28. What percentage of those with substance abuse problems had been attending school? _____%

29. For those attending school, were the schools generally aware of a substance abuse problem?
    1. ___ Yes
    2. ___ No

30. What percentage of those with a substance abuse problem had been enrolled in any substance abuse program before they came to the shelter/program?
    _____%

Services and Coordination with Other Providers Serving Youth

We would like to understand the types of services you provide and whether there are any referral patterns or special community coordination mechanisms that help you. We are especially interested in substance abuse prevention and intervention services for runaway and homeless youth.

31. How do runaway and homeless youth receive your services? Check all that apply.
    1. ___ By referral
    2. ___ Self-referral
    3. ___ Word of mouth (go to question 33)
    4. ___ Direct pick-up (go to question 33)
    5. ___ Other (please specify) (go to question 33) _____

32. For those who are referred, who makes the referral? Check all that apply.
    01. ___ Schools
    02. ___ Monitored work program
    03. ___ Community or neighborhood services (please specify) _____
    04. ___ Prior foster family or group home
    05. ___ Drug and rehabilitation programs
    06. ___ Health provider
    07. ___ Public social services program (please specify)_____
    08. ___ Hotline
    09. ___ Shelter/program outreach
    10. ___ Community education/outreach program
    11. ___ Juvenile justice system
    12. ___ Law enforcement system
    13. ___ Other (please specify) _____

33. Do you conduct assessments of youth when they come to you for services?
    1. ___ Yes
    2. ___ No (go to question 35)

34. If yes, please check the types of assessment you do. Check all that apply.

    How important is the assessment to your ability to intervene/prevent alcohol and drug abuse? Circle answer.

		Very Important	Somewhat Important	Not Very Important
1. ___	For drug abuse problems	1	2	3
2. ___	For alcohol abuse problems	1	2	3
3. ___	To identify any health problems, including HIV infection	1	2	3
4. ___	To identify any mental health problems	1	2	3

		How important is the assessment to your ability to intervene/prevent alcohol and drug abuse? Circle answer.		
		Very Important	**Somewhat Important**	**Not Very Important**
5. ___	To identify suicidal ideation	1	2	3
6. ___	For availability of help from nearby relatives or friends	1	2	3
7. ___	Other (please specify)	1	2	3

35. What is the average length of services to youth, including aftercare?
    1. ___ Less than one week
    2. ___ One to two weeks
    3. ___ Two weeks to one month
    4. ___ More than one month

36. Do youth who are ready for transition to independent living more frequently stay in your shelter or in a host home?
    1. ___ Shelter
    2. ___ Host home

37. Do youth who are ready for transition to independent living, *who also have a problem with alcoholism or drug abuse*, more frequently stay in your shelter or in a host home?
    1. ___ Shelter
    2. ___ Host home

38. What percentage of your clients are from your local area (within 50 miles)? _____%

39. Please indicate roughly what percentage of your shelter, host home, and other youth clients experienced the following problems last year:

Problem	Percent with Problem
01. Parent temporarily lost job	_____
02. Family temporarily lost housing	_____
03. Family with long-term economic problems	_____
04. Absence of caretaker	_____
05. Sexual abuse of youth by parent	_____
06. Other abuse of youth by parent	_____
07. Violence by other family members	_____
08. Parent has disability	_____
09. Parent has mental health problem	_____
10. Parent is an alcoholic	_____
11. Parent is a drug abuser	_____
12. Youth has education/school problems	_____

Problem	Percent with Problem
13. Youth has disability	_____
14. Youth has mental health problem	_____
15. Youth is an alcoholic	_____
16. Youth is a drug abuser	_____
17. Youth has attempted suicide	_____
18. Youth is in trouble with the justice system	_____
19. Youth is gay/lesbian	_____
20. Youth has AIDS or is HIV-positive	_____
21. Absence of mother	_____
22. Absence of father	_____
23. Youth has no means of support	_____
24. Youth was in foster care	_____
25. Other (please specify)	_____

40. Please indicate roughly what percentage of your youth clients have more than one of these problems.
   01. ___ More than 90%
   02. ___ 80%–90%
   03. ___ 70%–79%
   04. ___ 60%–69%
   05. ___ 50%–59%
   06. ___ 40%–49%
   07. ___ 30%–39%
   08. ___ 20%–29%
   09. ___ 10%–19%
   10. ___ Less than 10%

41. Have the types of problems faced by youth clients changed significantly over the last five years?
   1. ___ Yes
   2. ___ No (go to question 43)

42. If yes, please check all explanations that apply.
   01. ___ More long-term economic problems
   02. ___ More physical abuse by parent or caretaker
   03. ___ More sexual abuse by parent or caretaker
   04. ___ More parental drug abuse
   05. ___ More drug abuse among youth
   06. ___ More parental alcoholism
   07. ___ More alcoholism among youth
   08. ___ More parental health problems
   09. ___ More health problems among youth
   10. ___ More parental mental health problems

11. ___ More mental health problems among youth
12. ___ Youth have more school-related problems
13. ___ More homeless families
14. ___ Less coordination of services
15. ___ Other (please specify)_____

43. What was the destination of the youth clients who left your program last year? *Please indicate/estimate the percentage leaving for each destination.*
    01. ___% Parent's or guardian's home
    02. ___% Household of other parent figure
    03. ___% Relative's home
    04. ___% Friend's home
    05. ___% Foster home
    06. ___% Group home
    07. ___% Correctional facility
    08. ___% Independent/transitional living
    09. ___% Back to the street
    10. ___% Other (please specify) _____
    99. ___% Do not know

44. What was the destination of youth for whom independent/transitional living would be the appropriate plan? *Please indicate/estimate the percentage leaving for each destination.*
    01. ___% Parent's or guardian's home
    02. ___% Household of other parent figure
    03. ___% Relative's home
    04. ___% Friend's home
    05. ___% Foster home
    06. ___% Group home
    07. ___% Correctional facility
    08. ___% Independent/transitional living
    09. ___% Back to the street
    10. ___% Other (please specify) _____
    99. ___% Do not know

45. Was the destination of youth ready for transitional living affected by alcoholism or drug abuse?
    1. ___ Yes
    2. ___ No (go to question 47)

46. If yes, please explain.

Client outcome

47. During the last 12 months, what percentage of the youth in your program achieved the goals that they established with you? _____%

48. During the last 12 months, in your opinion what percentage of the youth in your program achieved satisfactory living arrangements after receiving your services? _____%

49. Do you provide follow-up to former youth clients?
    1. ___ Yes
    2. ___ No (go to question 54)

50. What percentage of the youth in your program maintained their goals six months after receiving your services? _____%

51. What percentage of the youth in your program maintained their goals 12 months after receiving your services? _____%

52. In your opinion, what percentage of the youth in your program maintained a satisfactory living arrangement six months after receiving your services? _____%

53. In your opinion, what percentage of the youth in your program maintained a satisfactory living arrangement 12 months after receiving your services? _____%

Public Awareness and Community Outreach

54. Has your community done anything to increase public awareness about the problems that cause youth to run away or the needs of runaway and homeless youth?
    1. ___ Yes
    2. ___ No (go to question 56)

55. Please identify the types of activities your community conducted to increase public awareness about the problems that cause youth to run away or the needs of runaway and homeless youth. Check all that apply.
    1. ___ Conducted sessions in schools
    2. ___ Distributed information in schools
    3. ___ Public service announcements on television
    4. ___ Public service announcements on radio
    5. ___ Other (please describe)_____

56. Has your community done any outreach to get runaway and homeless youth to avail themselves of community services?
    1. ___ Yes
    2. ___ No (go to question 58)
57. If yes, please identify the types of outreach your community used. Check all that apply.
    1. ___ Street workers
    2. ___ Counselors/workers in schools (working on individual basis)
    3. ___ Other (please describe)_____

    _____

Income Sources

There is increasing concern about the adequacy of resources and services to prevent substance abuse (and diseases contracted through substance abuse) among runaway and homeless youth. It would be most helpful if you would provide some information about any special financial support you received last year for treatment/prevention of alcohol and drug abuse.

58. Do you have any special grants or contracts to provide services to youth who are drug abusers or alcoholics, or to prevent substance abuse among youth?
    1. ___ Yes
    2. ___ No (go to question 60)

59. If yes, please list all grants and contracts dealing with substance abuse among youth, the funding source, and their dollar amounts. Please attach a brief description of each.

Grants and Contracts

Grant/Contract	Funding Source	Dollar Amount
_____	_____	_____
_____	_____	_____
_____	_____	_____
_____	_____	_____
_____	_____	_____
_____	_____	_____
_____	_____	_____

Exemplary Programs

60. Are there any features of your programs for youth that you consider exemplary?
    1. ___ Yes
    2. ___ No (go to question 62)

61. If yes, please describe them and explain why you consider them exemplary.

_____
_____
_____
_____
_____
_____

62. Name three programs serving runaway and homeless youth in transition to independent living that you consider exemplary and explain why. Please provide a contact person and telephone number for each.

_____
_____
_____
_____
_____
_____

63. Please identify three programs that have exemplary peer counseling support for youth and explain why you consider them exemplary. Please provide a contact person and telephone number for each.

_____
_____
_____
_____
_____
_____

Thank you.

B State Summaries of Provider Responses

STATES AND TERRITORIES WITH NO RESPONDENTS OR ONE RESPONDENT (NOT SUMMARIZED)

States with No Respondents

Alaska
District of Columbia
Hawaii
Nevada
New Mexico
North Dakota
Rhode Island
South Carolina
South Dakota
Utah

States with One Respondent

Delaware
Guam
Idaho
Louisiana
Maryland
Mississippi
Montana
Nebraska
Puerto Rico
Vermont
Virgin Islands
West Virginia
Wyoming

Note: Only responses with significant percentages are included in these summaries.

ALABAMA

Number of Providers Reporting:	2
Primary Description of Services:	Emergency Shelter
Type of Agency:	Nonprofit (2)
Usual Number of Residential Facilities:	No Usual; 1 (1), 3 (1)*
Do Providers Use Host Homes:	No

*Services Provided by 90%
or More of the Providers:*
(n = 2)

Outreach (2)
Screening/Intake (2)
Temporary Shelter (2)
Provide Meals (2)
Case Management (2)
Information and Referral (2)
Refer for Individual Counseling (2)
Provide Individual Counseling (2)
Refer to Family Counseling (2)
Provide Family Counseling (2)
Provide Transportation (2)
Refer for Health Care (2)
Refer to Aftercare Services (2)
Provide Aftercare Services (2)
Refer to Drug Abuse Program (2)
Refer to Program for Alcoholics (2)
Refer for Mental Health Services (2)
Refer for Treatment for Suicidal Behavior (2)
Refer to Develop Independent Living Plan (2)
Provide Independent Living Skills Training (2)
Provide Recreational Program (2)
Refer to Educational Program/GED (2)
Provide Advocacy for Clients (2)
Coordinate with Criminal/Juvenile Justice System (2)
Provide AIDS/HIV Education (2)
Refer for Recreation/Leisure Time Activities (2)

Common Aftercare Services:
(n = 2)

Individual Counseling (2)
Parent Counseling (2)
Family Counseling (2)

Common Problems Facing Youth: Insufficient Responses

*Destination of Clients Who
Left Program:*
(n = 2)

Parent's or Guardian's Home (58%)
Foster Home (16%)
Group Home (16%)
Back to the Street (10%)

---

*Numbers not in parentheses are number of facilities. Numbers in parentheses are number of respondents.

ARIZONA

Number of Providers Reporting:	2
Primary Description of Services:	Emergency Shelter and Transitional Housing (2)
Type of Agency:	Nonprofit (2)
Usual Number of Residential Facilities:	No Usual; 3 (1), 6 (1)*
Do Providers Use Host Homes:	No

Services Provided by 90%
or More of the Providers:
(n = 2)

Outreach (2)
Screening/Intake (2)
Temporary Shelter (2)
Case Management (2)
Information and Referral (2)
Follow-up to Referral (2)
Refer for Individual Counseling (2)
Provide Individual Counseling (2)
Refer to Family Counseling (2)
Provide Family Counseling (2)
Refer for Transportation (2)
Refer for Health Care (2)
Provide Transitional Living Beyond Shelter (2)
Refer for Other Living Arrangements (2)
Organize Other Living Arrangements (2)
Refer to Aftercare Services (2)
Provide Aftercare Services (2)
Refer to Drug Abuse Program (2)
Refer to Program for Alcoholics (2)
Refer for Mental Health Services (2)
Refer for Treatment for Suicidal Behavior (2)
Help Youth Develop Independent Living Plan (2)
Provide Independent Living Skills Training (2)
Provide Recreational Program (2)
Refer to Educational Program/GED (2)
Provide Advocacy for Clients (2)
Coordinate with Criminal/Juvenile Justice System (2)
Refer for AIDS/HIV Treatment (2)
Refer Gay/Lesbian Youth for Special Services (2)
Sponsor Recreation/Leisure Time Activities (2)
Refer for Recreation/Leisure Time Activities (2)

Common Aftercare Services:
(n = 2)

Case Management (2)
Individual Counseling (2)
Family Counseling (2)
Group Counseling (2)

Common Problems Facing Youth:

Youth Has Education/School Problems (70%)
Youth Has No Means of Support (58%)

Family Has Long Term Economic Problems (55%)
Other (Not Sexual) Abuse of Youth by Parent (55%)
Absence of Father (55%)
Absence of Caretaker (50%)
Youth Is in Trouble with the Justice System (45%)
Parent Temporarily Lost Job (40%)
Family Temporarily Lost Housing (40%)
Youth Has Mental Health Problem (40%)
Youth Is an Alcoholic (40%)
Sexual Abuse of Youth by Parent (38%)
Violence by Other Family Members (35%)
Youth Has Attempted Suicide (33%)
Parent Has Mental Health Problem (28%)
Parent Is an Alcoholic (28%)
Parent Is a Drug Abuser (28%)

Destination of Clients Who
Left Program:
(n = 2)

Parent's or Guardian's Home (45%)
Friend's Home (20%)
Foster Home (20%)
Relative's Home (13%)

ARKANSAS

Number of Providers Reporting: 4

Primary Description of Services: Emergency Shelter (all); Transitional Housing (1)

Type of Agency: Nonprofits (all)

Usual Number of Residential Facilities: No Usual; Range 1–5

Do Providers Use Host Homes: No (all)

Services Provided by 90%
or More of the Providers:
(n = 4)

Screening/Intake (4)
Temporary Shelter (4)
Provide Meals (4)
Case Management (4)
Information and Referral (4)
Refer for Individual Counseling (4)
Provide Individual Counseling (4)
Refer to Family Counseling (4)
Provide Family Counseling (4)
Provide Transportation (4)
Refer for Health Care (4)
Refer to Transitional Living Beyond Shelter (4)
Refer for Other Living Arrangements (4)
Provide Aftercare Services (4)
Refer to Drug Abuse Program (4)
Refer to Program for Alcoholics (4)

Refer for Mental Health Services (4)
Refer for Treatment for Suicidal Behavior (4)
Provide Recreational Program (4)
Refer to Educational Program/GED (4)
Provide Advocacy for Clients (4)
Coordinate with Criminal/Juvenile Justice System (4)

Common Aftercare Services:
(n = 4)

Case Management (4)
Individual Counseling (4)
Parent Counseling (4)
Family Counseling (4)

Common Problems Facing Youth:
(n = 3)

Youth Has Education/School Problems (57%)
Family with Long-Term Economic Problems (45%)
Other (Not Sexual) Abuse of Youth by Parent (45%)
Youth Is in Trouble with the Justice System (42%)
Absence of Father (42%)
Youth Has Mental Health Problem (37%)
Violence by Other Family Members (31%)
Absence of Caretaker (28%)
Parent Is an Alcoholic (28%)
Parent Has Mental Health Problem (27%)
Sexual Abuse of Youth by Parent (25%)

Destination of Clients Who
Left Program:
(n = 3)

Parent's or Guardian's Home (55%)
Group Home (10%)
Foster Home (9%)
Relative's Home (5%)
Correctional Facility (5%)

CALIFORNIA

Number of Providers Reporting: 16

Primary Description of Services: Emergency Shelter (all)

Type of Agency: Nonprofit (all)

Usual Number of Residential Facilities: 1 (13 out of 16)

Do Providers Use Host Homes: No (all)

Services Provided by 90%
or More of the Providers:
(n = 16)

Outreach (16)
Screening/Intake (16)
Information & Referral (16)
Provide Individual Counseling (16)
Provide Family Counseling (16)
Help Youth Develop Independent Living Plan (16)
Refer to Educational Program/GED (16)

Temporary Shelter (15)
Provide Meals (15)
Case Management (15)
Refer to Drug Abuse Program (15)
Refer to Program for Alcoholics (15)
Refer for Treatment for Suicidal Behavior (15)
Provide Advocacy for Clients (15)

Common Aftercare Services:
(n = 15)

Counseling for Alcoholism (15)
Counseling for Drug Abuse (15)
Individual Counseling (15)
Family Counseling (15)
Mental Health Services (14)
Group Counseling (14)
Case Management (13)
Education (13)
Job Training (13)
Parent Counseling (13)

Common Problems Facing Youth:
(n = 14)

Youth Has Education/School Problem (69%)
Other (Not Sexual) Abuse of Youth by Parent (57%)
Absence of Father (50%)
Family Has Long-Term Economic Problems (46%)
Youth Was in Foster Care (45%)
Youth Has No Means of Support (45%)
Sexual Abuse of Youth by Parent (39%)
Parent Is an Alcoholic (35%)
Violence by Other Family Members (32%)
Youth Is a Drug Abuser (32%)
Youth Has Attempted Suicide (32%)
Youth Has a Mental Health Problem (31%)
Youth Is in Trouble with the Justice System (30%)
Parent Is a Drug Abuser (29%)
Absence of Caretaker (26%)

Destination of Clients Who
Left Program:
(n = 15)

Parent or Guardian's Home (57%)
Independent/Transitional Living (14%)
Do Not Know (12%)
Back to the Street (11%)

COLORADO

Number of Providers Reporting: 5

Primary Description of Services: Emergency Shelter (all); Housing for Emancipated
Youth (2); Transitional Housing (1)

Type of Agency: 4 Nonprofits; 1 Public

Usual Number of Residential Facilities: No Usual; Range 1–5

Do Providers Use Host Homes: 4 No; 1 Yes

Services Provided by 90%
or More of the Providers:
(n = 5)

Screening/Intake (5)
Temporary Shelter (5)
Provide Meals (5)
Case Management (5)
Information and Referral (5)
Provide Individual Counseling (5)
Refer to Family Counseling (5)
Provide Family Counseling (5)
Provide Transportation (5)
Refer to Drug Abuse Program (5)
Refer to Program for Alcoholics (5)
Provide Recreational Program (5)
Provide Advocacy for Clients (5)
Coordinate with Criminal/Juvenile Justice System (5)

Common Aftercare Services:
(n = 4)

Case Management (4)
Counseling for Alcoholism (4)
Counseling for Drug Abuse (4)
Individual Counseling (4)
Family Counseling (4)
Recreation/Leisure Time Activities (4)

Common Problems Facing Youth:
(n = 5)

Youth Has Education/School Problems (70%)
Absence of Father (53%)
Family with Long-Term Economic Problems (48%)
Youth Has No Means of Support (46%)
Absence of Caretaker (45%)
Other (Not Sexual) Abuse of Youth by Parent (41%)
Youth Is in Trouble with the Justice System (37%)
Youth Was in Foster Care (37%)
Youth Has Attempted Suicide (33%)
Parent Is an Alcoholic (29%)
Violence by Other Family Members (27%)

Destination of Clients Who
Left Program:
(n = 5)

Parent's or Guardian's Home (46%)
Back to the Street (15%)
Other, varied (15%)
Group Home (10%)
Foster Home (5%)
Independent/Transitional Living (5%)

CONNECTICUT

Number of Providers Reporting: 4

Primary Description of Services: Emergency Shelter (all); Transitional Housing (1)

Type of Agency:	Nonprofits (all)
Usual Number of Residential Facilities:	1 (all)
Do Providers Use Host Homes:	3 No; 1 Yes

Services Provided by 90%
or More of the Providers:
(n = 4)

Outreach (4)
Screening/Intake (4)
Temporary Shelter (4)
Provide Meals (4)
Case Management (4)
Information and Referral (4)
Follow-up to Referral (4)
Provide Individual Counseling (4)
Provide Transportation (4)
Refer for Health Care (4)
Refer for Other Living Arrangements (4)
Refer to Drug Abuse Program (4)
Refer to Program for Alcoholics (4)
Refer for Mental Health Services (4)
Refer for Treatment for Suicidal Behavior (4)
Refer for Employment Assistance (4)
Provide Advocacy for Clients (4)
Coordinate with Criminal/Juvenile Justice System (4)
Provide AIDS/HIV Education (4)
Refer Gay/Lesbian Youth for Special Services (4)

Common Aftercare Services:
(n = 4)

Family Counseling (4)
Group Counseling (4)
Case Management (3)
Health Care (3)
Education (3)
Job Training (3)
Counseling for Alcoholism (3)
Counseling for Drug Abuse (3)
Mental Health Services (3)
Individual Counseling (3)

Common Problems Facing Youth:
(n = 4)

Absence of Father (53%)
Youth Has No Means of Support (50%)
Parent Is a Drug Abuser (40%)
Youth Is a Drug Abuser (39%)
Family with Long-Term Economic Problems (38%)
Violence by Other Family Members (33%)
Parent Temporarily Lost Job (25%)
Other (Not Sexual) Abuse of Youth by Parent (25%)

Destination of Clients Who
Left Program:
(n = 4)

Parent's or Guardian's Home (58%)
Group Home (13%)
Independent/Transitional Living (13%)
Household of Other Parent Figure (9%)

FLORIDA

Number of Providers Reporting:	15
Primary Description of Services:	Emergency Shelter (14 out of 15)
Type of Agency:	14 Nonprofits; 1 Public
Usual Number of Residential Facilities:	1 (10 out of 15)
Do Providers Use Host Homes:	No (14 out of 15)

Services Provided by 90%
or More of the Providers:
(n = 15)

Case Management (15)
Information & Referral (15)
Provide Individual Counseling (15)
Refer to Drug Abuse Program (15)
Refer to Program for Alcoholics (15)
Provide Recreational Program (15)
Outreach (14)
Screening/Intake (14)
Provide Meals (14)
Follow-up to Referral (14)
Refer for Individual Counseling (14)
Refer to Family Counseling (14)
Provide Family Counseling (14)
Refer for Health Care (14)
Refer for Treatment for Suicidal Behavior (14)
Coordinate with Criminal/Juvenile Justice (14)

Common Aftercare Services:
(n = 14)

Family Counseling (13)
Individual Counseling (12)
Case Management (11)
Group Counseling (11)
Parent Counseling (10)
Mental Health Services (10)

Common Problems Facing Youth:
(n = 12)

Youth Has Education/School Problems (66%)
Absence of Father (44%)
Other (Not Sexual) Abuse by Parent (40%)
Family Has Long-Term Economic Problems (38%)
Violence by Other Family Members (38%)
Youth Has No Means of Support (37%)
Parent Is an Alcoholic (32%)
Youth Is in Trouble with Justice System (27%)
Parent Is a Drug Abuser (26%)
Youth Was in Foster Care (25%)

Destination of Clients Who
Left Program:
(n = 13)

Parent's or Guardian's Home (53%)
Foster Home (12%)
Household of Other Parent Figure (11%)
Group Home (11%)
Back to the Street (11%)

GEORGIA

Number of Providers Reporting:	3
Primary Description of Services:	Emergency Services (all); Transitional Housing/ Housing for Emancipated Youth (1)
Type of Agency:	Nonprofit (all)
Usual Number of Residential Facilities:	1
Do Providers Use Host Homes:	1 Yes; 2 No

Services Providers by 90% or More of the Providers: (n = 3)

Screening/Intake (3)
Temporary Shelter (3)
Provide Meals (3)
Case Management (3)
Information and Referral (3)
Follow-up to Referral (3)
Refer for Individual Counseling (3)
Provide Individual Counseling (3)
Refer to Family Counseling (3)
Provide Family Counseling (3)
Refer for Health Care (3)
Refer to Aftercare Services (3)
Provide Aftercare Services (3)
Refer to Drug Abuse Program (3)
Refer for Mental Health Services (3)
Refer for Treatment for Suicidal Behavior (3)
Provide Recreational Program (3)
Provide Advocacy for Clients (3)
Refer to Agency That Will Serve as Advocate (3)
Coordinate with Criminal Juvenile Justice System (3)
Provide AIDS/HIV Education (3)

Common Aftercare Services: (n = 3)

Counseling for Alcoholism (3)
Individual Counseling (3)
Parent Counseling (3)
Family Counseling (3)
Group Counseling (3)

Common Problems Facing Youth: (n = 3)

Youth has Education/School Problems (76%)
Other (Not Sexual) Abuse of Youth by Parent (73%)
Family with Long-Term Economic Problems (55%)
Absence of Father (51%)
Youth Was in Foster Care (43%)
Parent Is an Alcoholic (38%)
Violence by Other Family Members (33%)
Parent Is a Drug Abuser (33%)
Youth Has No Means of Support (29%)

Sexual Abuse of Youth by Parent (28%)
Parent Has Mental Health Problem (27%)

Destination of Clients Who	Parent's or Guardian's Home (38%)
Left Program:	Foster Home (24%)
(n = 3)	Group Home (15%)
	Relative's Home (9%)

ILLINOIS

Number of Providers Reporting:	6
Primary Description of Services:	Emergency Shelter (6)
	Transitional Housing (2)
Type of Agency:	Nonprofits (all)
Usual Number of Residential Facilities:	1 or 2
Do Providers Use Host Homes:	4 No; 2 Yes

Services Provided by 90%	Screening/Intake (6)
or More of the Providers:	Temporary Shelter (6)
(n = 6)	Information and Referral (6)
	Provide Individual Counseling (6)
	Refer for Other Living Arrangements (6)
	Refer to Drug Abuse Program (6)
	Provide Recreational Program (6)
	Provide Advocacy for Clients (6)
	Coordinate with Criminal/Juvenile Justice (6)

Common Aftercare Services:	Parent Counseling (5)
(n = 5)	Family Counseling (5)
	Case Management (4)
	Counseling for Alcoholism (4)
	Counseling for Drug Abuse (4)
	Mental Health Services (4)
	Individual Counseling (4)

Common Problems Facing Youth:	Family with Long-Term Economic Problems (58%)
(n = 5)	Youth Has Education/School Problems (57%)
	Other (Not Sexual) Abuse of Youth by Parent (50%)
	Absence of Father (50%)
	Violence by Other Family Members (48%)
	Sexual Abuse of Youth by Parent (46%)
	Parent Is an Alcoholic (39%)
	Youth Has No Means of Support (39%)
	Youth Is Gay/Lesbian (35%)

Parent Has a Mental Health Problem (32%)
Parent Temporarily Lost Job (30%)
Family Temporarily Lost Housing (30%)
Parent Is a Drug Abuser (26%)
Youth Is a Drug Abuser (25%)
Youth Has Mental Health Problem (22%)

Destination of Clients Who Parent's or Guardian's Home (45%)
Left Program: Independent/Transitional Living (27%)
(n = 6) Foster Home (21%)

INDIANA

Number of Providers Reporting: 5

Primary Description of Services: Emergency Services (all); Transitional Housing (1)

Type of Agency: Nonprofit (all)

Usual Number of Residential Facilities: 1 (all)

Do Providers Use Host Homes: No (all)

Services Provided by 90% Outreach (5)
or More of the Providers: Screening/Intake (5)
(n = 5) Temporary Shelter (5)
Provide Meals (5)
Case Management (5)
Information and Referral (5)
Refer for Individual Counseling (5)
Provide Individual Counseling (5)
Refer to Family Counseling (5)
Refer to Drug Abuse Program (5)
Refer to Program for Alcoholics (5)
Refer for Mental Health Services (5)
Refer for Treatment for Suicidal Behavior (5)
Coordinate with Criminal/Juvenile Justice System (5)
Provide AIDS/HIV Education (5)

Common Aftercare Services: Individual Counseling (4)
(n = 4) Parent Counseling (4)
Family Counseling (4)

Common Problems Facing Youth: Parent Temporarily Lost Job (60%)
(n = 5) Youth Has Education/School Problem (59%)
Other (Not Sexual) Abuse of Youth by Parent (55%)
Parent Is a Drug Abuser (54%)
Absence of Father (54%)
Parent Is an Alcoholic (48%)

Youth Has Disability (44%)
Youth Is in Trouble with the Justice System (44%)
Family with Long-Term Economic Problems (42%)
Sexual Abuse of Youth by Parent (35%)
Youth Has Mental Health Problem (34%)
Violence by Other Family Member (33%)
Parent Has Mental Health Problem (32%)
Youth Has Attempted Suicide (32%)
Family Temporarily Lost Housing (30%)
Youth Is a Drug Abuser (27%)

Destination of Clients Who   Parent's or Guardian's Home (55%)
Left Program: Household of Other Parent Figure (17%)
(n = 5)   Foster Home (16%)
Group Home (13%)

IOWA

Number of Providers Reporting: 6

Primary Description of Services: Emergency Shelter (4); Transitional Housing (2);
Housing for Emancipated Youth (2); Other Services
(3)

Type of Agency: Nonprofits (all)

Usual Number of Residential Facilities: No Usual; Range 2–6

Do Providers Use Host Homes: 5 No; 1 Yes

Services Provided by 90%   Outreach (6)
or More of the Providers: Screening/Intake (6)
(n = 6)   Case Management (6)
Provide Individual Counseling (6)
Provide Family Counseling (6)
Provide Recreational Program (6)
Coordinate with Criminal/Juvenile Justice System (6)

Common Aftercare Services: Group Counseling (6)
(n = 6)   Case Management (5)
Job Training (5)
Mental Health Services (5)
Individual Counseling (5)
Peer Counseling (5)

Common Problems Facing Youth: Other, No Pattern (58%)
(n = 6)   Youth Has Education/School Problems (55%)
Youth Is an Alcoholic (47%)
Absence of Father (46%)

Other (Not Sexual) Abuse of Youth by Parent (43%)
Absence of Caretaker (42%)
Youth Is a Drug Abuser (42%)
Violence by Other Family Members (38%)
Youth Has Mental Health Problems (37%)
Family with Long-Term Economic Problems (36%)
Parent Is an Alcoholic (30%)
Youth Has Attempted Suicide (30%)
Parent Is a Drug Abuser (29%)
Youth Was in Foster Care (27%)

Destination of Clients Who   Parent's or Guardian's Home (41%)
Left Program: Independent/Transitional Living (21%)
(n = 6)   Group Home (18%)
                                 Foster Home (11%)
                                 Back to the Street (11%)

KANSAS

Number of Providers Reporting: 2

Primary Description of Services: Emergency Shelter (2); Transitional Housing (1)

Type of Agency: Nonprofit (2)

Usual Number of Residential Facilities: No Usual; 1 reports 6

Do Providers Use Host Homes: 1 Yes; 1 No

Services Provided by 90%   Outreach (2)
or More of the Providers: Screening/Intake (2)
(n = 2)   Temporary Shelter (2)
                                 Provide Meals (2)
                                 Case Management (2)
                                 Information and Referral (2)
                                 Follow-up to Referral (2)
                                 Provide Individual Counseling (2)
                                 Provide Family Counseling (2)
                                 Refer to Transitional Living Beyond Shelter (2)
                                 Refer for Other Living Arrangements (2)
                                 Provide Aftercare Services (2)
                                 Refer to Drug Abuse Program (2)
                                 Refer for Mental Health Services (2)
                                 Refer for Treatment for Suicidal Behavior (2)
                                 Help Youth Develop Independent Living Plan (2)
                                 Provide Independent Living Skills Training (2)
                                 Provide Recreational Program (2)
                                 Refer to Educational Program/GED (2)
                                 Refer for Employment Assistance (2)

Refer to Agency that will serve as Advocate (2)
Coordinate with Criminal/Juvenile Justice System (2)
Provide AIDS/HIV Education (2)

Common Aftercare Services: Case Management (2)
(n = 2)

Common Problems Facing Youth: Insufficient Responses

Destination of Clients Who   Insufficient Responses
Left Program:

KENTUCKY

Number of Providers Reporting: 2

Primary Description of Services: Emergency Shelter (both); Transitional Housing (1)

Type of Agency: For Profit (1); Non Profit (1)

Usual Number of Residential Facilities: No Usual; 3 (1)*

Do Providers Use Host Homes: Yes (both)

Services Provided by 90%   Screening/Intake (2)
or More of the Providers: Temporary Shelter (2)
(n = 2)   Case Management (2)
                                     Information and Referral (2)
                                     Follow-up to Referral (2)
                                     Refer for Individual Counseling (2)
                                     Provide Individual Counseling (2)
                                     Refer to Family Counseling (2)
                                     Provide Family Counseling (2)
                                     Refer for Health Care (2)
                                     Provide Aftercare Services (2)
                                     Refer for Treatment for Suicidal Behavior (2)
                                     Provide Educational Program/GED (2)
                                     Refer for Employment Assistance (2)
                                     Coordinate with Criminal/Juvenile Justice System (2)
                                     Provide AIDS/HIV Education (2)
                                     Refer for AIDS/HIV Treatment (2)
                                     Refer Minority/Immigrant Youth to Special Services (2)

Common Aftercare Services: Case Management (2)
(n = 2)   Health Care (2)
                                     Job Training (2)
                                     Employment (2)
                                     Counseling for Alcoholism (2)
                                     Counseling for Drug Abuse (2)

Mental Health Services (2)
Individual Counseling (2)
Parent Counseling (2)
Family Counseling (2)
Group Counseling (2)
Alternative Living (2)

Common Problems Facing Youth:
(n = 2)

Youth Has Education/School Problems (75%)
Youth Is in Trouble with the Justice System (73%)
Parent Temporarily Lost Job (60%)
Youth Has Mental Health Problem (58%)
Youth Has no Means of Support (58%)
Family Has Long Term Economic Problems (53%)
Youth Is an Alcoholic (40%)
Youth Is a Drug Abuser (40%)
Youth Was in Foster Care (35%)
Other (Not Sexual) Abuse of Youth by Parent (33%)
Violence by Other Family Members (30%)
Parent Is an Alcoholic (28%)
Absence of Father (25%)

Destination of Clients Who
Left Program:
(n = 2)

Parent's or Guardian's Home (73%)
Group Home (15%)

MAINE

Number of Providers Reporting: 2

Primary Description of Services: Emergency Shelter (2); Transitional Housing (1)

Type of Agency: Nonprofit (2)

Usual Number of Residential Facilities: No Usual; 1 (1), 3 (1)*

Do Providers Use Host Homes: No

Services Provided by 90%
or More of the Providers:
(n = 2)

Screening/Intake (2)
Temporary Shelter (2)
Arrange for Meals (2)
Provide Meals (2)
Information and Referral (2)
Follow-up to Referral (2)
Refer for Individual Counseling (2)
Provide Individual Counseling (2)
Refer to Family Counseling (2)
Provide Family Counseling (2)
Refer for Health Care (2)
Refer to Transitional Living Beyond Shelter (2)

Refer for Other Living Arrangements (2)
Refer to Aftercare Services (2)
Provide Aftercare Services (2)
Refer to Drug Abuse Program (2)
Refer for Mental Health Services (2)
Refer for Treatment for Suicidal Behavior (2)
Refer to Develop Independent Living Plan (2)
Provide Recreational Program (2)
Refer to Recreational Program (2)
Refer for Employment Assistance (2)
Provide Advocacy for Clients (2)
Coordinate with Criminal/Juvenile Justice System (2)
Provide AIDS/HIV Education (2)

Common Aftercare Services:
(n = 2)

Counseling for Alcoholism (2)
Counseling for Drug Abuse (2)
Mental Health Services (2)
Individual Counseling (2)
Parent Counseling (2)
Family Counseling (2)
Group Counseling (2)
Alternative Living (2)
Financial Assistance (2)
Recreational/Leisure Time Activities (2)

Common Problems Facing Youth:
(n = 2)

Youth Has no Means of Support (95%)
Absence of Father (90%)
Youth Has Education/School Problems (93%)
Youth Has Mental Health Problem (85%)
Youth Has Disability (80%)
Absence of Caretaker (78%)
Family with Long Term Economic Problems (75%)
Parent Is an Alcoholic (75%)
Parent Is a Drug Abuser (75%)
Youth Was in Foster Care (68%)
Sexual Abuse of Youth by Parent (63%)
Violence by Other Family Members (60%)
Parent Temporarily Lost Job (55%)
Parent Has Mental Health Problem (55%)
Youth Is an Alcoholic (53%)
Other (Not Sexual) Abuse of Youth by Parent (48%)
Youth Has Attempted Suicide (40%)
Youth Is in Trouble with the Justice System (40%)
Absence of Mother (35%)
Youth Is a Drug Abuser (30%)

Destination of Clients Who
Left Program:
(n = 2)

Foster Home (33%)
Parent's or Guardian's Home (28%)
Household of Other Parent Figure (18%)
Correctional Facility (10%)
Independent/Transitional Living (8%)

MASSACHUSETTS

Number of Providers Reporting:	3
Primary Description of Services:	Emergency Services (all); Transitional Housing (1)
Type of Agency:	Nonprofits (all)
Usual Number of Residential Facilities:	1 (1); 5 (1)*
Do Providers Use Host Homes:	2 No; 1 Yes

Services Provided by 90%
or More of the Providers:
(n = 3)

Screening/Intake (3)
Temporary Shelter (3)
Provide Meals (3)
Case Management (3)
Information and Referral (3)
Refer for Individual Counseling (3)
Provide Individual Counseling (3)
Refer to Family Counseling (3)
Provide Family Counseling (3)
Refer for Health Care (3)
Refer to Transitional Living Beyond Shelter (3)
Refer for Other Living Arrangements (3)
Refer to Aftercare (3)
Refer to Drug Abuse Program (3)
Refer to Program for Alcoholics (3)
Provide Mental Health Services (3)
Refer for Mental Health Services (3)
Refer for Treatment for Suicidal Behavior (3)
Provide Independent Living Skills Training (3)
Provide Recreational Program (3)
Provide Educational Program/GED (3)
Provide Advocacy for Clients (3)
Coordinate with Criminal/Juvenile Justice System (3)
Provide AIDS/HIV Education (3)
Sponsor Recreational/Leisure Time Activities (3)

Common Aftercare Services:
(n = 2)

Health Care (2)
Mental Health Services (2)
Individual Counseling (2)
Parent Counseling (2)
Family Counseling (2)
Group Counseling (2)
Peer Counseling (2)
Alternative Living (2)
Recreation/Leisure Time Activities (2)

Common Problems Facing Youth: Insufficient Responses

Destination of Clients Who *Left Program:* *(n = 3)*	Parent's or Guardian's Home (37%) Foster Home (14%) (Remainder 5% or 3%)

MICHIGAN

Number of Providers Reporting:	5
Primary Description of Services:	Emergency Shelter (all); 1 Transitional Housing and Housing for Emancipated Youth
Type of Agency:	5 nonprofits
Usual Number of Residential Facilities:	1 (4); 2 (1)*
Do Providers Use Host Homes:	No (all)

Services Provided by 90%
or More of the Providers:
(n = 5)

Outreach (5)
Screening/Intake (5)
Temporary Shelter (5)
Provide Meals (5)
Case Management (5)
Information and Referral (5)
Refer for Individual Counseling (5)
Provide Individual Counseling (5)
Provide Family Counseling (5)
Refer to Aftercare Services (5)
Help Youth Develop Independent Living Plan (5)
Provide Independent Living Skills Training (5)
Coordinate with Criminal Juvenile Justice System (5)
Provide AIDS/HIV Education (5)

Common Aftercare Services:
(n = 4)

Case Management (4)
Education (4)
Counseling for Drug Abuse (4)
Mental Health Services (4)
Individual Counseling (4)
Parent Counseling (4)
Family Counseling (4)
Group Counseling (4)

Common Problems Facing Youth:
(n – 4)

Youth Has No Means of Support (65%)
Parent Is an Alcoholic (62%)
Youth Has Education/School Problems (61%)
Youth Is in Trouble with the Justice System (49%)
Absence of Father (48%)
Family with Long-Term Economic Problems (40%)
Other (Not Sexual) Abuse of Youth by Parent (40%)
Parent Is a Drug Abuser (38%)

Youth Is a Drug Abuser (38%)
Violence by Other Family Members (35%)
Youth Has Attempted Suicide (28%)
Youth Was in Foster Care (28%)

Destination of Clients Who
Left Program:
(n = 4)

Parent's or Guardian's Home (59%)
Household of Other Parent Figure (16%)
Foster Home (13%)
Independent/Transitional Living (6%)
Relative's Home (5%)

MINNESOTA

Number of Providers Reporting: 5

Primary Description of Services: Emergency Shelter (all)

Type of Agency: Nonprofits (all)

Usual Number of Residential Facilities: 1 (all)

Do Providers Use Host Homes: 3 No; 2 Yes

Services Provided by 90%
or More of the Providers:
(n = 5)

Outreach (5)
Screening/Intake (5)
Temporary Shelter (5)
Provide Meals (5)
Information and Referral (5)
Provide Individual Counseling (5)
Provide Transportation (5)
Refer for Other Living Arrangements (5)
Refer to Drug Abuse Program (5)
Refer to Program for Alcoholics (5)
Refer to Educational Program/GED (5)
Provide Advocacy for Clients (5)

Common Aftercare Services:
(n = 5)

Case Management (5)
Counseling for Alcoholism (5)
Counseling for Drug Abuse (5)
Mental Health Services (5)
Individual Counseling (5)
Family Counseling (5)
Group Counseling (5)

Common Problems Facing Youth:
(n = 5)

Family with Long-Term Economic Problems (61%)
Other, No Pattern (60%)
Youth Has Education/School Problem (46%)
Absence of Father (39%)
Other (Not Sexual) Abuse of Youth by Parent (35%)

Parent Is an Alcoholic (33%)
Youth Was in Foster Care (27%)

Destination of Clients Who
Left Program:
(n = 5)

Parent's or Guardian's Home (55%)
Foster Home (12%)
Back to the Street (10%)
Relative's Home (6%)
Group Home (5%)
Other, varied (5%)

MISSOURI

Number of Providers Reporting: 3

Primary Description of Services: Emergency Shelter (all); Transitional Housing (1);
Housing for Emancipated Youth (1)

Type of Agency: Nonprofits (all)

Usual Number of Residential Facilities: 2 (2); 3 (1)*

Do Providers Use Host Homes: No (all)

Services Provided by 90%
or More of the Providers:
(n = 3)

Screening/Intake (3)
Temporary Shelter (3)
Provide Meals (3)
Case Management (3)
Information and Referral (3)
Provide Individual Counseling (3)
Refer to Family Counseling (3)
Refer for Health Care (3)
Refer to Drug Abuse Program (3)
Refer to Program for Alcoholics (3)
Refer for Mental Health Services (3)
Refer for Treatment for Suicidal Behavior (3)
Provide Recreational Program (3)
Refer for Employment Assistance (3)
Provide AIDS/HIV Education (3)

Common Aftercare Services:
(n = 2)

Case Management (2)
Health Care (2)
Education (2)
Job Training (2)
Employment (2)
Counseling for Alcoholism (2)
Counseling for Drug Abuse (2)
Mental Health Services (2)
Individual Counseling (2)
Parent Counseling (2)

Family Counseling (2)
Group Counseling (2)
Peer Counseling (2)
Alternative Living (2)
Financial Assistance (2)

Common Problems Facing Youth: Youth Has Education/School Problems (84%)
(n = 3)   Other (Not Sexual) Abuse of Youth by Parent (64%)
Absence of Father (63%)
Family with Long-Term Economic Problems (58%)
Youth Was in Foster Care (45%)
Youth Has No Means of Support (44%)
Sexual Abuse of Youth by Parent (41%)
Youth Is in Trouble with the Justice System (40%)
Parent Is an Alcoholic (34%)
Youth Is a Drug Abuser (27%)

Destination of Clients Who   Parent's or Guardian's Home (21%)
Left Program: Household of Other Parent Figure (19%)
(n = 3)   Relative's Home (18%)
Independent/Transitional Living (18%)
Group Home (16%)

NEW HAMPSHIRE

Number of Providers Reporting: 2

Primary Description of Services: Emergency Shelter

Type of Agency: Nonprofit (2)

Usual Number of Residential Facilities: No Usual; 1 (1); 3 (1)*

Do Providers Use Host Homes: 1 Yes; 1 No

Services Provided by 90%   Screening/Intake (2)
or More of the Providers: Temporary Shelter (2)
(n = 2)   Provide Meals (2)
Case Management (2)
Information and Referral (2)
Follow-up to Referral (2)
Refer for Individual Counseling (2)
Provide Individual Counseling (2)
Provide Family Counseling (2)
Refer for Health Care (2)
Refer for Other Living Arrangements (2)
Provide Aftercare Services (2)
Refer to Drug Abuse Program (2)
Refer for Mental Health Services (2)

Help Youth Develop Independent Living Plan (2)
Provide Independent Living Skills Training (2)
Provide Recreational Program (2)
Refer to Educational Program/GED (2)
Refer for Employment Assistance (2)
Provide Advocacy for Clients (2)
Coordinate with Criminal/Juvenile Justice System (2)
Sponsor Recreational/Leisure Time Activities (2)
Refer for Recreation/Leisure Time Activities (2)

Common Aftercare Services:
(n = 2)

Case Management (2)
Health Care (2)
Education (2)
Job Training (2)
Employment (2)
Counseling for Alcoholism (2)
Counseling for Drug Abuse (2)
Mental Health Services (2)
Individual Counseling (2)
Parent Counseling (2)
Family Counseling (2)
Group Counseling (2)
Peer Counseling (2)
Alternative Living (2)
Recreation/Leisure Time Activities (2)

Common Problems Facing Youth:
(n = 2)

Youth Has Education/School Problems (58%)
Absence of Father (40%)
Family Has Long-Term Economic Problems (38%)
Other (Not Sexual) Abuse of Youth by Parent (38%)
Parent Is an Alcoholic (38%)
Youth Is an Alcoholic (33%)
Absence of Caretaker (30%)
Youth Is a Drug Abuser (29%)
Absence of Mother (28%)
Youth Is in Trouble with the Justice System (27%)
Violence by Other Family Members (26%)
Parent Has Mental Health Problem (25%)

Destination of Clients Who
Left Program:
(n = 2)

Parent's or Guardian's Home (58%)
Group Home (10%)
Independent/Transitional Living (10%)
Correctional Facility (8%)
Household of Other Parent Figure (6%)

New Jersey

Number of Providers Reporting: 7

Primary Description of Services: Emergency Shelter (all); Transitional Housing (3)

Type of Agency:	6 Nonprofits; 1 Public
Usual Number of Residential Facilities:	1–3
Do Providers Use Host Homes:	6 No; 1 Yes

Services Provided by 90%
or More of the Providers:
(n = 7)

Outreach (7)
Screening/Intake (7)
Case Management (7)
Information and Referral (7)
Provide Individual Counseling (7)
Provide Family Counseling (7)
Provide Transportation (7)
Provide Aftercare Services (7)
Refer to Educational Program/GED (7)

Common Aftercare Services:
(n = 5)

Individual Counseling (5)
Case Management (4)
Education (4)
Counseling for Alcoholism (4)
Counseling for Drug Abuse (4)
Mental Health Services (4)
Recreation/Leisure Time Activities (4)

Common Problems Facing Youth:
(n = 7)

Youth Has Education/School Problems (52%)
Youth Has No Means of Support (47%)
Youth Has Mental Health Problem (41%)
Absence of Father (39%)
Family with Long-Term Economic Problems (26%)
Youth Was in Foster Care (26%)

Destination of Clients Who
Left Program:
(n = 7)

Parent's or Guardian's Home (60%)
Foster Home (11%)
Relative's Home (9%)
Group Home (8%)
Back to Street (8%)

NEW YORK

Number of Providers Reporting:	6
Primary Description of Services:	Emergency Shelter (6)
Type of Agency:	Nonprofit (6)
Usual Number of Residential Facilities:	No usual, ranges from 0 to 4
Do Providers Use Host Homes:	No (6)

Services Provided by 90% *or More of the Providers:* *(n = 6)*	Screening/Intake (6) Temporary Shelter (6) Provide Meals (6) Case Management (6) Information and Referral (6) Provide Individual Counseling (6) Provide Family Counseling (6) Refer for Health Care (6) Refer for Other Living Arrangements (6) Refer to Drug Abuse Program (6) Refer to Program for Alcoholics (6) Refer for Mental Health Services (6) Provide Independent Living Skills Training (6) Refer for Employment Assistance (6)
Common Aftercare Services: *(n = 6)*	Case Management (6) Individual Counseling (6) Family Counseling (6) Health Care (5) Education (5) Job Training (5) Counseling for Alcoholism (5) Counseling for Drug Abuse (5) Group Counseling (5)
Common Problems Facing Youth: *(n = 6)*	Youth Has Education/School Problems (62%) Family Has Long-Term Economic Problems (51%) Other (Not Sexual) Abuse by Parent (47%) Violence by Other Family Members (46%) Absence of Father (44%)
Destination of Clients Who *Left Program:* *(n = 6)*	Parent's or Guardian's Home (51%) Household of Other Parent Figure (14%) Foster Home (12%) Independent/Transitional Living (12%) Relative's Home (10%)

NORTH CAROLINA

Number of Providers Reporting:	4
Primary Description of Services:	Emergency Services (all); Transitional Housing (2); Housing for Emancipated Youth (1)
Type of Agency:	3 Nonprofits; 1 Public
Usual Number of Residential Facilities:	1 (3); 5 (1)*
Do Providers Use Host Homes:	No (all)

Services Provided by 90%
or More of the Providers:
(n = 4)

Outreach (4)
Screening/Intake (4)
Temporary Shelter (4)
Provide Meals (4)
Case Management (4)
Information and Referral (4)
Follow-Up to Referral (4)
Provide Individual Counseling (4)
Provide Family Counseling (4)
Provide Transportation (4)
Refer for Health Care (4)
Provide Aftercare Services (4)
Refer to Drug Abuse Program (4)
Refer for Mental Health Services (4)
Refer for Treatment for Suicidal Behavior (4)
Provide Recreational Program (4)
Refer to Educational Program/GED (4)
Provide Advocacy for Clients (4)

Common Aftercare Services:
(n = 4)

Case Management (4)
Health Care (4)
Counseling for Drug Abuse (4)
Mental Health Services (4)
Individual Counseling (4)
Parent Counseling (4)
Family Counseling (4)

Common Problems Facing Youth:
(n = 4)

Absence of Father (66%)
Youth Has Education/School Problems (58%)
Family with Long-Term Economic Problems (50%)
Youth Is in Trouble with the Justice System (36%)
Youth Has Attempted Suicide (34%)
Youth Is an Alcoholic (33%)
Parent Is an Alcoholic (32%)
Other (Not Sexual) Abuse of Youth by Parent (29%)
Parent Is a Drug Abuser (26%)
Youth Has Mental Health Problem (25%)

Destination of Clients Who
Left Program:
(n = 4)

Parent's or Guardian's Home (54%)
Back to the Street (11%)
Friend's Home (10%)
Group Home (9%)
Relative's Home (8%)

OHIO

Number of Providers Reporting: 3

Primary Description of Services: Emergency Shelter (all)

Type of Agency:	Nonprofit (all)
Usual Number of Residential Facilities:	1 (all)
Do Providers Use Host Homes:	No (all)

Services Provided by 90% *or More of the Providers:* *(n = 3)*	Outreach (3) Screening/Intake (3) Temporary Shelter (3) Provide Meals (3) Case Management (3) Information and Referral (3) Follow-up to Referral (3) Refer for Individual Counseling (3) Provide Individual Counseling (3) Refer to Family Counseling (3) Provide Family Counseling (3) Provide Transportation (3) Refer for Health Care (3) Organize Other Living Arrangements (3) Refer to Aftercare Services (3) Provide Aftercare Services (3) Refer to Drug Abuse Program (3) Refer for Mental Health Services (3) Provide Treatment for Suicidal Behavior (3) Refer for Treatment of Suicidal Behavior (3) Provide Recreational Program (3) Refer for Employment Assistance (3) Provide Advocacy for Clients (3) Sponsor Peer Counseling (3) Provide AIDS/HIV Education (3)
Common Aftercare Services: *(n = 3)*	Case Management (3) Individual Counseling (3) Family Counseling (3) Financial Assistance (3)
Common Problems Facing Youth: *(n = 3)*	Youth Has Attempted Suicide (48%) Other (Not Sexual) Abuse of Youth by Parent (45%) Sexual Abuse of Youth by Parent (35%) Youth Is an Alcoholic (32%) Youth Has Mental Health Problem (26%) Youth Is a Drug Abuser (25%)
Destination of Clients Who *Left Program:* *(n = 3)*	Parent's or Guardian's Home (54%) Relative's Home (15%) Back to the Street (12%) Unknown (9%)

OKLAHOMA

Number of Providers Reporting: 4

Primary Description of Services: Emergency Shelter (all)

Type of Agency: Nonprofits (all)

Usual Number of Residential Facilities: 1 (all)

Do Providers Use Host Homes: 3 No; 1 Yes

Services Provided by 90%   Screening/Intake (4)
or More of the Providers: Temporary Shelter (4)
(n = 4)   Provide Meals (4)
                                          Case Management (4)
                                          Information and Referral (4)
                                          Provide Individual Counseling (4)
                                          Provide Family Counseling (4)
                                          Refer to Drug Abuse Program (4)
                                          Refer for Treatment for Suicidal Behavior (4)
                                          Coordinate with Criminal/Juvenile Justice System (4)

Common Aftercare Services: Individual Counseling (4)
(n = 4)   Counseling for Alcoholism (3)
                                          Counseling for Drug Abuse (3)
                                          Family Counseling (3)
                                          Group Counseling (3)

Common Problems Facing Youth: Absence of Father (80%)
(n = 3)   Youth Has Education/School Problem (55%)
                                          Other—Severe Neglect, Law Violation (53%)
                                          Family with Long-Term Economic Problems (49%)
                                          Youth Is in Trouble with the Justice System (38%)
                                          Youth Is a Drug Abuser (35%)

Destination of Clients Who   Parent's or Guardian's Home (57%)
Left Program: Foster Home (25%)
(n = 4)   Household of Other Parent Figure (15%)

OREGON

Number of Providers Reporting: 4

Primary Description of Services: Emergency Shelter (all); Transitional Housing (2)

Type of Agency: Nonprofits (all)

Usual Number of Residential Facilities: 1

Do Providers Use Host Homes:	Yes (all)
Services Provided by 90% *or More of the Providers:* *(n = 4)*	Screening/Intake (4) Temporary Shelter (4) Provide Meals (4) Case Management (4) Information and Referral (4) Provide Family Counseling (4) Refer for Health Care (4) Refer to Drug Abuse Program (4) Refer to Program for Alcoholics (4) Refer for Mental Health Services (4) Refer for Treatment for Suicidal Behavior (4) Help Youth Develop Independent Living Plan (4) Refer to Educational Program/GED (4) Refer for Employment Assistance (4) Refer Minority/Immigrant Youth (with language and cultural barriers) to Special Services
Common Aftercare Services: *(n = 4)*	Case Management (3) Individual Counseling (3) Family Counseling (3) Alternative Living (3)
Common Problems Facing Youth: *(n = 3)*	Youth Has Education/School Problem (88%) Absence of Father (75%) Youth Has No Means of Support (75%) Youth Is in Trouble with the Justice System (65%) Other (Not Sexual) Abuse of Youth by Parent (52%) Family with Long-Term Economic Problems (48%) Sexual Abuse of Youth by Parent (42%) Violence by Other Family Members (42%) Youth Has Mental Health Problem (38%) Absence of Caretaker (35%) Parent Is an Alcoholic (35%) Parent Is a Drug Abuser (35%) Parent Has Mental Health Problem (33%) Youth Was in Foster Care (33%) Youth Is an Alcoholic (29%) Youth Is a Drug Abuser (29%)
Destination of Clients Who *Left Program:*	Insufficient Responses

PENNSYLVANIA

Number of Providers Reporting:	8
Primary Description of Services:	Emergency Shelter (8)

Transitional Housing (2)
Housing for Emancipated Youth (1)

Type of Agency: Nonprofit (all)

Usual Number of Residential Facilities: No usual number; Range 1–8

Do Providers Use Host Homes: 3 No; 4 Yes

Services Provided by 90%
or More of the Providers:
(n = 8)

Outreach (8)
Screening/Intake (8)
Temporary Shelter (8)
Information and Referral (8)
Provide Individual Counseling (8)
Refer to Drug Abuse Program (8)
Refer to Program for Alcoholics (8)
Coordinate with Criminal/Juvenile Justice (8)

Common Aftercare Services:
(n = 7)

Individual Counseling (7)
Case Management (6)
Family Counseling (6)
Counseling for Alcoholism (5)
Counseling for Drug Abuse (5)
Parent Counseling (5)

Common Problems Facing Youth:
(n = 7)

Absence of Father (57%)
Family Has Long-Term Economic Problems (56%)
Youth Has Education/School Problems (54%)
Youth Has No Means of Support (46%)
Parent Temporarily Lost Job (37%)
Youth Has Mental Health Problem (35%)
Youth Has Disability (32%)
Youth Is in Trouble with the Justice System (29%)
Absence of Caretaker (28%)
Youth Was in Foster Care (27%)
Parent Has Mental Health Problem (24%)
Parent Is an Alcoholic (24%)
Other (Not Sexual) Abuse of Youth by Parent (23%)

Destination of Clients Who
Left Program:
(n = 8)

Parent's or Guardian's Home (64%)
Foster Home (18%)
Do Not Know (13%)

TENNESSEE

Number of Providers Reporting: 3

Primary Description of Services: Emergency Shelter (all) and Transitional Housing (all)

Type of Agency:	Nonprofits (all)
Usual Number of Residential Facilities:	1 (1); 2 (1); 6 (1)*
Do Providers Use Host Homes:	No (all)

Services Provided by 90%
or More of the Providers:
(n = 3)

Outreach (3)
Screening/Intake (3)
Temporary Shelter (3)
Provide Meals (3)
Case Management (3)
Information and Referral (3)
Follow-up to Referral (3)
Refer for Individual Counseling (3)
Provide Individual Counseling (3)
Refer to Family Counseling (3)
Provide Family Counseling (3)
Provide Transportation (3)
Refer for Health Care (3)
Refer to Transitional Living Beyond Shelter (3)
Refer for Other Living Arrangements (3)
Refer to Aftercare Services (3)
Provide Aftercare Services (3)
Refer to Drug Abuse Program (3)
Refer to Program for Alcoholics (3)
Refer for Mental Health Services (3)
Refer for Treatment for Suicidal Behavior (3)
Provide Independent Living Skills Training (3)
Provide Recreational Program (3)
Refer to Educational Program/GED (3)
Refer for Employment Assistance (3)
Provide Advocacy for Clients (3)
Coordinate with Criminal/Juvenile Justice System (3)
Provide AIDS/HIV Education (3)
Refer Minority/Immigrant Youth (with Language and
Cultural Barriers) to Special Services (3)
Sponsor Recreation/Leisure Time Activities (3)

Common Aftercare Services:
(n = 3)

Health Care (3)
Counseling for Drug Abuse (3)
Individual Counseling (3)

Common Problems Facing Youth: Insufficient Responses

Destination of Clients Who
Left Program:
(n = 3)

Parent's or Guardian's Home (33%)
Group Home (11%)
Back to the Street (10%)
Other, Varied (10%)
Correctional Facility (9%)
Foster Home (8%)
Relative's Home (7%)

TEXAS

Number of Providers Reporting:	7
Primary Description of Services:	Emergency Shelter (all)
Type of Agency:	6 Nonprofits; 1 Public
Usual Number of Residential Facilities:	2 or 3
Do Providers Use Host Homes:	6 No; 1 Yes

*Services Provided by 90%
or More of the Providers:
(n = 7)*

Temporary Shelter (7)
Provide Meals (7)
Refer for Individual Counseling (7)
Refer to Family Counseling (7)
Refer for Health Care (7)
Refer to Drug Abuse Program (7)
Refer for Mental Health Services (7)
Refer for Treatment for Suicidal Behavior (7)
Coordinate with Criminal/Juvenile Justice (7)

*Common Aftercare Services:
(n = 6)*

Case Management (6)
Employment (5)
Individual Counseling (5)

*Common Problems Facing Youth:
(n = 6)*

Youth Has Education/School Problems (57%)
Other (Not Sexual) Abuse of Youth by Parent (56%)
Absence of Father (53%)
Family Has Long-Term Economic Problems (41%)
Sexual Abuse of Youth by Parent (37%)
Parent Is an Alcoholic (36%)
Youth Has No Means of Support (34%)
Youth Is in Trouble with the Justice System (33%)
Youth Has Mental Health Problem (31%)
Youth Was in Foster Care (31%)

*Destination of Clients Who
Left Program:
(n = 7)*

Parent's or Guardian's Home (49%)
Other (27%)
Group Home (12%)
Foster Home (9%)
Household of Other Parent Figure (8%)

VIRGINIA

Number of Providers Reporting:	6
Primary Description of Services:	Emergency Shelter (all)

Type of Agency:	5 nonprofit; 1 public
Usual Number of Residential Facilities:	1
Do Providers Use Host Homes:	3 no; 3 yes

Services Provided by 90%
or More of the Providers:
(n = 6)

Temporary Shelter (6)
Information and Referral (6)
Refer for Individual Counseling (6)
Refer to Family Counseling (6)
Provide Transportation (6)
Refer to Drug Abuse Program (6)
Provide Recreational Program (6)

Common Aftercare Services:
(n = 3)

Financial Assistance (3)

Common Problems Facing Youth:
(n = 5)

Youth has Education/School Problems (51%)
Other (Not Sexual) Abuse of Youth by Parents (42%)
Absence of Father (38%)
Absence of Caregiver (32%)
Youth Is in Trouble with the Justice System (30%)
Parent Is an Alcoholic (27%)
Youth Has No Means of Support (26%)
Sexual Abuse of Youth by Parent (25%)
Violence by Other Family Members (20%)
Youth Was in Foster Care (19%)

Destination of Clients Who
Left Program:
(n = 6)

Parent's or Guardian's Home (58%)
Group Home (12%)
Other (12%)
Foster Home (10%)

WASHINGTON

Number of Providers Reporting:	4
Primary Description of Services:	Emergency Shelter (all); Transitional Housing (2)
Type of Agency:	Nonprofit (all)
Usual Number of Residential Facilities:	No usual, Range 1–4
Do Providers Use Host Homes:	2 Yes; 1 No

Services Provided by 90%
or More of the Providers:
(n = 4)

Outreach (4)
Screening/Intake (4)
Temporary Shelter (4)
Provide Meals (4)

Case Management (4)
Information and Referral (4)
Refer for Individual Counseling (4)
Provide Individual Counseling (4)
Refer to Family Counseling (4)
Provide Family Counseling (4)
Refer for Health Care (4)
Refer to Transitional Living Beyond Shelter (4)
Organize Other Living Arrangements (4)
Refer to Aftercare Services (4)
Provide Aftercare Services (4)
Refer for Mental Health Services (4)
Refer for Treatment for Suicidal Behavior (4)
Provide Recreational Program (4)
Provide Advocacy for Clients (4)
Coordinate with Criminal/Juvenile Justice System (4)
Provide AIDS/HIV Education (4)

Common Aftercare Services:
(n = 4)

Individual Counseling (4)
Case Management (3)
Health Care (3)
Education (3)
Job Training (3)
Employment (3)
Counseling for Alcoholism (3)
Counseling for Drug Abuse (3)
Mental Health Services (3)
Group Counseling (3)
Alternative Living (3)
Financial Assistance (3)

Common Problems Facing Youth:
(n = 4)

Youth Has No Means of Support (76%)
Youth Has Education/School Problems (73%)
Family Has Long-Term Economic Problems (58%)
Absence of Father (56%)
Other (Not Sexual) Abuse of Youth by Parent (51%)
Youth Is a Drug Abuser (45%)
Absence of Caretaker (38%)
Sexual Abuse of Youth by Parent (38%)
Parent Is an Alcoholic (33%)
Youth Has Attempted Suicide (30%)
Parent Is a Drug Abuser (27%)
Youth Was in Foster Care (25%)

Destination of Clients Who
Left Program:
(n = 4)

Parent's or Guardian's Home (38%)
Group Home (17%)
Back to the Street (14%)
Foster Home (11%)
Other, Varied (11%)

WISCONSIN

Number of Providers Reporting:	2
Primary Description of Services:	Emergency Shelter
Type of Agency:	Nonprofit (2)
Usual Number of Residential Facilities:	1
Do Providers Use Host Homes:	No

Services Provided by 90%
or More of the Providers:
(n = 2)

Outreach (2)
Screening/Intake (2)
Temporary Shelter (2)
Arrange for Meals (2)
Provide Meals (2)
Case Management (2)
Information and Referral (2)
Provide Individual Counseling (2)
Provide Family Counseling (2)
Refer for Other Living Arrangements (2)
Refer to Drug Abuse Program (2)
Refer to Program for Alcoholics (2)
Provide Mental Health Services (2)
Refer for Treatment for Suicidal Behavior (2)
Refer to Educational Program/GED (2)
Provide Advocacy for Clients (2)
Coordinate with Criminal/Juvenile Justice System (2)
Sponsor Peer Counseling (2)
Provide AIDS/HIV Education (2)
Refer Gay/Lesbian Youth for Special Services (2)
Provide Special Services to Minority and Immigrant Youth (2)

Common Aftercare Services:
(n = 2)

Individual Counseling (2)
Parent Counseling (2)
Family Counseling (2)

Common Problems Facing Youth:
(n = 2)

Family Has Long-Term Economic Problems (78%)
Youth Has Education/School Problems (46%)
Parent Is an Alcoholic (41%)
Other (Not Sexual) Abuse of Youth by Parent (35%)
Youth Has Mental Health Problem (35%)
Absence of Father (33%)
Sexual Abuse of Youth by Parent (31%)
Violence by Other Family Members (25%)
Parent Is a Drug Abuser (25%)

Destination of Clients Who
Left Program:
(n = 2)

Parent's or Guardian's Home (61%)
Household of Other Parent Figure (10%)
Relative's Home (7%)
Foster Home (6%)
Group Home (5%)
Correctional Facility (5%)
Independent/Transitional Living (5%)

Independent Living Survey Instrument and Methodology

The grant awarded to the National Association of Social Workers (NASW) proposed a survey of state independent living coordinators. NASW received responses from 14 coordinators (out of 51), or a 28 percent response. Three other states provided information about their programs although they did not complete the survey form. Because the large states (for example, New York, California, and Texas) did not respond to the survey questions, the data are not representative of independent living programs throughout the country. Consequently, project staff did not adjust the data. The data represent only those states that responded to the survey. Data from the 1990 Census show, however, that the states responding to the independent living survey have 27 percent of the children under age 18 in the United States and represent eight of the 10 Department of Health and Human Services (HHS) regions. These states and their populations are identified below.

State	Population Under Age 18	HHS Region No.
Illinois	2,946,366	5
Pennsylvania	2,794,810	3
New Jersey	1,799,462	2
Georgia	1,727,307	4
Tennessee	1,216,604	4
Minnesota	1,166,783	5
Maryland	1,163,241	3
Arizona	981,119	9
South Carolina	920,207	4
Colorado	861,266	8
New Mexico	446,741	6
Utah	627,444	8
New Hampshire	278,755	1
Wyoming	135,525	8
Total	17,065,630 (27%)	

Note: Total 1990 census of children under age 18 in United States = 63,503,692.

Questionnaire
INDEPENDENT LIVING SERVICES FOR YOUTH

Name and Title of Person Responding: Telephone #:

Agency: State:

Agency and Program Characteristics

We are trying to identify key elements that help you respond to the needs of youth who are ready for independent living, including agency characteristics, the services available to youth, and the training you give staff who provide independent living services. We especially want to know which elements enhance the ability of providers to intervene or prevent substance abuse among youth.

1. How many independent living providers does your state have? Please provide actual number. _____

2. How many youth did these providers serve during the last 12 months? Please provide estimated number served. _____

3. Which of the following services do independent living providers in your state offer to youth? Check all that apply.

How important are these services to intervention/prevention of alcohol and drug abuse? Circle answer.

		Very Important	Somewhat Important	Not Very Important
01. ___	Outreach	1	2	3
02. ___	Screening/intake	1	2	3
03. ___	Temporary shelter	1	2	3
04. ___	Arrange for meals	1	2	3
05. ___	Provide meals	1	2	3
06. ___	Case management	1	2	3
07. ___	Information and referral	1	2	3
08. ___	Refer for individual counseling	1	2	3
09. ___	Provide individual counseling	1	2	3
10. ___	Refer for family counseling	1	2	3
11. ___	Provide family counseling	1	2	3
12. ___	Refer for transportation	1	2	3
13. ___	Provide transportation	1	2	3
14. ___	Refer for health care	1	2	3
15. ___	Provide health care	1	2	3
16. ___	Refer to transitional living beyond shelter	1	2	3
17. ___	Provide transitional living beyond shelter	1	2	3
18. ___	Refer for other living arrangements	1	2	3

Which of the following services do independent living providers in your state offer to youth? Check all that apply.

How important are these services to intervention/prevention of alcohol and drug abuse? Circle answer.

	Very Important	Somewhat Important	Not Very Important
19. ___ Organize other living arrangements	1	2	3
20. ___ Refer to aftercare services	1	2	3
21. ___ Provide aftercare services	1	2	3
22. ___ Test for substance abuse	1	2	3
23. ___ Refer to drug abuse program	1	2	3
24. ___ Provide drug abuse program (please attach a brief description)	1	2	3
25. ___ Refer to program for alcoholics	1	2	3
26. ___ Provide program for alcoholics (please attach a brief description)	1	2	3
27. ___ Provide mental health services	1	2	3
28. ___ Refer for mental health services	1	2	3
29. ___ Provide treatment for suicidal behavior	1	2	3
30. ___ Refer for treatment for suicidal behavior	1	2	3
31. ___ Refer to develop independent living plan	1	2	3
32. ___ Help youth develop independent living plan	1	2	3
33. ___ Provide independent living skills training	1	2	3
34. ___ Refer for independent living skills training	1	2	3
35. ___ Provide recreational program	1	2	3
36. ___ Refer to recreational program	1	2	3
37. ___ Provide educational program/ general equivalency diploma	1	2	3
38. ___ Refer to educational program/general equivalency diploma	1	2	3
39. ___ Provide employment assistance	1	2	3
40. ___ Refer for employment assistance	1	2	3

Which of the following services do independent living providers in your state offer to youth? Check all that apply.

How important are these services to intervention/prevention of alcohol and drug abuse? Circle answer.

		Very Important	Somewhat Important	Not Very Important
41. ___	Provide advocacy for clients	1	2	3
42. ___	Refer to agency that will serve as advocate	1	2	3
43. ___	Coordinate with criminal/ juvenile justice system	1	2	3
44. ___	Refer to agency that coordinates with criminal/juvenile justice system	1	2	3
45. ___	Sponsor peer counseling	1	2	3
46. ___	Refer for peer counseling	1	2	3
47. ___	Provide AIDS/HIV education	1	2	3
48. ___	Refer for AIDS/HIV treatment	1	2	3
49. ___	Provide special services to gay/lesbian youth	1	2	3
50. ___	Refer gay/lesbian youth for special services	1	2	3
51. ___	Provide special services to minority and immigrant youth (with language and cultural barriers)	1	2	3
52. ___	Refer minority/immigrant youth (with language and cultural barriers) to special services	1	2	3
53. ___	Sponsor recreation/leisure time activities	1	2	3
54. ___	Refer for recreation/leisure time activities	1	2	3
55. ___	Other (please specify)	1	2	3

_____

_____

_____

4. Please identify the aftercare services that you provide or to which you refer youth who are transitioning to independent living. Check all that apply.

How important are these services to intervention/prevention of alcohol and drug abuse? Circle answer.

		Very Important	Somewhat Important	Not Very Important
01. ___	Case management	1	2	3
02. ___	Health care	1	2	3

Please identify the aftercare services that you provide or to which you refer youth who are transitioning to independent living. Check all that apply.

How important are these services to intervention/prevention of alcohol and drug abuse? Circle answer.

	Very Important	Somewhat Important	Not Very Important
03. ___ Education	1	2	3
04. ___ Job training	1	2	3
05. ___ Employment	1	2	3
06. ___ Counseling for alcoholism	1	2	3
07. ___ Counseling for drug abuse	1	2	3
08. ___ Mental health services	1	2	3
09. ___ Individual counseling	1	2	3
10. ___ Parent counseling	1	2	3
11. ___ Family counseling	1	2	3
12. ___ Group counseling	1	2	3
13. ___ Peer counseling	1	2	3
14. ___ Alternative living	1	2	3
15. ___ Financial assistance	1	2	3
16. ___ Recreation/leisure time activities	1	2	3
17. ___ None	1	2	3
18 ___ Other (please specify)	1	2	3

_____

_____

Program Staff and Volunteers

We would like to understand how important your staffing is to the ability of independent living providers to intervene/prevent alcohol and drug abuse among youth. Please answer each question and circle how important the response is.

	Very Important	Somewhat Important	Not Very Important
5. Please estimate the average staff-to-client ratio in the independent living programs in your state. _____	1	2	3

6. What percentage of the staff providing independent living services to youth (full-time and part-time) has a bachelor's degree in—

		Very Important	Somewhat Important	Not Very Important
1. Social work	___%	1	2	3
2. Psychology	___%	1	2	3
3. Nursing	___%	1	2	3
4. Counseling	___%	1	2	3
5. Other (please specify)	___%	1	2	3

_____

_____

7. What percentage of the staff providing independent living services to youth (full-time and part-time) has a master's degree in—

How important are these services to intervention/prevention of alcohol or drug abuse? Circle answer.

		Very Important	Somewhat Important	Not Very Important
1. Social work	____%	1	2	3
2. Psychology	____%	1	2	3
3. Nursing	____%	1	2	3
4. Counseling	____%	1	2	3
5. Other (please specify)	____%	1	2	3

_____

_____

8. What percentage of the staff providing independent living services (full-time and part-time) does not have a college degree? _____%

1   2   3

9. Do you have a training program for staff providing independent living services to youth?
   1. ___ Yes
   2. ___ No (go to question 12)

10. What type of general training is available to the staff serving youth? Check all that apply.

How important is the training to the intervention/prevention of alcohol and drug abuse? Circle answer.

	Very Important	Somewhat Important	Not Very Important
1. ___ Orientation (one-half day or less)	1	2	3
2. ___ In-service training (special workshops or continuing education courses of one or more days)	1	2	3
3. ___ Initial work with supervisor	1	2	3
4. ___ None	1	2	3

11. What type of specialized training is available to the staff serving youth? Check all that apply.

| 1. ___ Special training on alcohol and drug abuse | 1 | 2 | 3 |
| 2. ___ Special training on mental health problems | 1 | 2 | 3 |

What type of specialized training is available to the staff serving youth? Check all that apply.

How important is the training to the intervention/prevention of alcohol and drug abuse? Circle answer.

		Very Important	Somewhat Important	Not Very Important
3. ___	Special training on suicidal behavior	1	2	3
4. ___	None	1	2	3
5. ___	Other (please specify)	1	2	3

_____

_____

Clients

We want to understand the roles of various types of agencies that serve different types of clients. The following questions will help us understand the types of youth served by independent living programs and any special problems they have.

12. What were the living situations for youth before they came to independent living programs in your state? Please indicate/estimate the percentage of youth from each living situation.

How important are these prior living situations to intervention/prevention of alcohol and drug abuse? Circle answer.

	Percent Living in Situation	Very Important	Somewhat Important	Not Very Important
01. Foster home	____%	1	2	3
02. Parents	____%	1	2	3
03. Relative	____%	1	2	3
04. Correctional facility	____%	1	2	3
05. Group home	____%	1	2	3
06. Independent living	____%	1	2	3
07. Runaway or crisis shelter	____%	1	2	3
08. Friend	____%	1	2	3
09. On the street	____%	1	2	3
10. Other (please specify)	____%	1	2	3

_____

_____

13. What percentage of the youth who had/have a substance abuse problem are—

1. White	____%	
2. Black	____%	
3. Hispanic	____%	
4. Asian	____%	
5. Other	____%	

14. What percentage of the youth who had/have a substance abuse problem are—
    1. Male   ____%
    2. Female   ____%

15. What percentage of those with substance abuse problems had been attending school?   _____%

16. For those attending school, were the schools generally aware of a substance abuse problem?
    1. ___ Yes
    2. ___ No

17. What percentage of those with a substance abuse problem had been enrolled in any substance abuse program before they came to the independent living programs in your state?   _____%

Services and Coordination with Other Providers Serving Youth
We would like to understand the types of services provided through your independent living programs and whether there are any referral patterns or special community coordination mechanisms that help. We are especially interested in substance abuse prevention and intervention services for youth in independent living programs.

18. How are youth referred to your state's programs? Check all that apply.
    01. ___ Schools
    02. ___ Monitored work program
    03. ___ Community or neighborhood services (please specify) _____

    04. ___ Prior foster family or group home
    05. ___ Drug and rehabilitation programs
    06. ___ Health provider
    07. ___ Public social services program (please specify) _____

    08. ___ Hotline
    09. ___ Shelter/program outreach
    10. ___ Community education/outreach program
    11. ___ Juvenile justice system
    12. ___ Law enforcement system
    13. ___ Other (please specify) _____

19. Do providers conduct assessment of youth when they come for services?
    1. ___ Yes
    2. ___ No (go to question 21)

20. Please check the types of assessment that providers do. Check all that apply.

    How important is the assessment to intervention/prevention of alcohol and drug abuse? Circle answer.

		Very Important	Somewhat Important	Not Very Important
1. ___	For drug abuse problems	1	2	3
2. ___	For alcohol abuse problems	1	2	3
3. ___	To identify any health problems, including HIV infection	1	2	3
4. ___	To identify any mental health problems	1	2	3
5. ___	To identify suicidal ideation	1	2	3
6. ___	For availability of help from nearby relatives or friends	1	2	3
7. ___	Other (please specify)	1	2	3

21. What is the average length of services to youth, including aftercare?
    1. ___ Less than one week
    2. ___ One to two weeks
    3. ___ Two weeks to one month
    4. ___ Six months
    5. ___ More than six months

22. Have the types of problems faced by youth clients changed significantly over the last five years?
    1. ___ Yes
    2. ___ No (go to question 24)

23. Please check all explanations that apply.
    01. ___ More long-term economic problems
    02. ___ More physical abuse by parent or caretaker
    03. ___ More sexual abuse by parent or caretaker
    04. ___ More parental drug abuse
    05. ___ More drug abuse among youth
    06. ___ More parental alcoholism
    07. ___ More alcoholism among youth
    08. ___ More parental health problems
    09. ___ More health problems among youth
    10. ___ More parental mental health problems
    11. ___ More mental health problems among youth
    12. ___ Youth have more school-related problems
    13. ___ More homeless families
    14. ___ Less coordination of services
    15. ___ Other (please specify) _____

24. What was the destination of youth leaving independent living programs in your state during the last 12 months? *Please indicate/estimate the percentage leaving for each destination.*
   01. _____% Parent's or guardian's home
   02. _____% Household of other parent figure
   03. _____% Relative's home
   04. _____% Friend's home
   05. _____% Foster home
   06. _____% Group home
   07. _____% Correctional facility
   08. _____% Independent/transitional living
   09. _____% Back to the street
   10. _____% Other (please specify) _____
   11. _____% Do not know

25. Was the destination environment for youth ready for transitional living affected by alcoholism or drug abuse?
   1. ___ Yes
   2. ___ No (go to question 27)

26. If yes, please explain. _____
   _____
   _____

Client Outcome

27. During the last 12 months, what percentage of the youth in your state's programs achieved the goals that they established in the independent living programs? _____%

28. During the last 12 months, in your opinion what percentage of the youth in your programs achieved satisfactory living arrangements after receiving independent living services? _____%

29. Do independent living providers in your state follow up with former youth clients?
   1. ___ Yes
   2. ___ No (go to question 34)

30. What percentage of youth in your state's programs maintained their goals six months after receiving your services? _____%

31. What percentage of youth in your state's programs maintained their goals 12 months after receiving your services? _____%

32. In your opinion, what percentage of youth in your state's programs maintained a satisfactory living arrangement six months after receiving your services? _____%

33. In your opinion, what percentage of youth in your state's programs maintained a satisfactory living arrangement 12 months after receiving your services?
_____%

Public Awareness and Community Outreach

34. Has your community done anything to increase public awareness about the needs of youth who are ready for independent living?
    1. ___ Yes
    2. ___ No (go to question 36)

35. Please identify the types of activities your community conducted to increase public awareness about the needs of youth who are ready for independent living. Check all that apply.
    1. ___ Conducted sessions in schools
    2. ___ Distributed information in schools
    3. ___ Public service announcements on television
    4. ___ Public service announcements on radio
    5. ___ Other (please describe) _____

Income Sources

There is increasing concern about the adequacy of resources and services to prevent substance abuse (and diseases contracted through substance abuse) among youth. It would be most helpful if you would provide some information about any special financial support your independent living programs received last year for treatment/prevention of alcohol and drug abuse.

36. Do your independent living providers have any special grants or contracts to provide services to youth who are drug abusers or alcoholics, or to prevent substance abuse among youth?
    1. ___ Yes
    2. ___ No (go to question 38)

37. Please list below each grant and contract dealing with substance abuse among youth, its dollar amount, and a brief description. If necessary, attach a separate sheet of paper with your descriptions.

Grant/Contract	Dollar Amount	Description
_____	_____	_____
_____	_____	_____
_____	_____	_____
_____	_____	_____
_____	_____	_____
_____	_____	_____

Exemplary Programs

38. Are there any features of your independent living programs that you consider exemplary?

    1. ___   Yes
    2. ___   No (go to question 40)

39. Please describe them and explain why you consider them exemplary.

    _____
    _____
    _____
    _____
    _____
    _____
    _____
    _____

40. Name three programs providing independent living services that you consider exemplary and explain why. Please provide a contact person and telephone number for each.

    _____
    _____
    _____
    _____
    _____
    _____
    _____
    _____

41. Please identify three programs that have exemplary peer counseling support for youth and explain why you consider them exemplary. Please provide a contact person and telephone number for each.

    _____
    _____
    _____
    _____
    _____
    _____
    _____

Thank you.

D *Examples of Assessment Instruments*

The Front Door
707 North Eighth Street
Columbia, Missouri 65201

INITIAL INTERVIEW OUTLINE

1. Client's Presenting Problem:
   A. Reason for admission _____

   B. Client's attempts to solve problem _____
   _____
   _____
   _____

2. Social History:
   A. Family
      1. Parents' marital status and current living arrangements. If client is an adult, inquire about client's status. _____
      _____
      _____

      2. Names and ages of siblings, their current placement and frequency of client contact with them _____
      _____

      3. When and why client stopped residing in the parental home _____
      _____
      _____

      4. Significant relatives, other than the family of origin _____
      _____
      _____

   B. Previous Placement
      1. type i.e. group home, foster home _____
      _____

    2. Duration _____

_____

_____

    3. Reason for termination _____

_____

_____

_____

_____

C. Peer Relations
    1. Descriptions of peer group _____

_____

    2. Peer group activities _____

_____

3. Educational History:
  A. Last grade completed _____
    1. Last school attended _____
    2. Level of performance _____
  B. Special Classes Attended e.g. BD, LD _____

_____

4. Vocational History:
  A. Previous work experience _____

_____

  B. Volunteer experience _____

_____

5. Legal Status
  A. Client's Guardian _____

_____

  B. Juvenile Court Intervention _____

_____

_____

6. Staff Assessment
  A. Behavior
    1. Appearance of being stoned, high or intoxicated _____

_____

_____

    2. Inactive or hyperactive _____

_____

  B. Thought Disorder
    1. Logical thought pattern _____

_____

    2. Able to focus attention on interview _____

3. Hears voices, possesses special powers _____

_____

_____

C. Sensorium
   1. Intact memory _____
   2. Oriented to time, place and person _____
D. Overall Impression
   1. Cooperative, manipulative, superficial, credible, suspicious, etc. _____

_____

_____

_____

7. Staff Formulation of Problem:
   A. Based on interview and other observation:

_____

_____

_____

_____

_____

   B. Compare with client's assessment of problem:

_____

_____

_____

_____

_____

INTAKE SHEET

Code #_____

Intake by_____

Assigned To_____ Date_____

Name _____ D.O.B. _____ School _____

Address _____ Age _____ Guidance/Grade _____

_____ Gender _____ Living w/ _____

Phone _____ Race/Ethnic _____

Parents:

_____Natural   _____Natural

_____Adoptive   Mother: _____   _____Adoptive   Father: _____

_____Step   Address: _____   _____Step   Address: _____

_____Foster   Phone: _____W   _____Foster   Phone: _____W

_____H   _____H

D.C.Y.S. Involvement: Yes_____   No_____

Status— Protective Services _____   Committed Delinquent _____

         Committed FWSN _____   Committed Abuse/Neglect _____

         Non-Committed_____

Court   Present _____   Past_____

Involvement: Adjudicated Delinquent _____   FWSN (Date) _____

               Accused Delinquent_____   Youthful Offender _____

               Probation Officer _____

Referral Source: _____   Phone_____

Name of Caller_____   Relationship to Client _____

Reason for Referral:

_____Runaway   _____Info/Advoc.   _____Crisis Intervention

_____Truancy   _____Homeless   _____Beyond Control

_____Abuse (Physical/Sex.)   _____Pushout/Throwout

Living Situation: _____

_____

_____

In Need of Placement: Yes_____   No_____

Precipitating Factors _____

_____

_____

_____

Personal: Assessment of Client

Describe appearance, eye contact, speech rate and quality, range of affect, mood, perceptual process, thought process and content, disturbances of appetite, and/or sleep.

_____

_____

_____

_____

_____

Please Check Area of Difficulty:

1. COGNITIVE:
_____a. thoughts incoherent
_____b. delusional
_____c. self destructive
_____d. overdeveloped fantasy life
_____e. confusion
_____f. learning disabled
_____g. very limited

2. SOMATIC:
_____a. chronic illness
type_____
_____b. frequent physical complaints
_____c. sleep disturbance
_____d. change in appetite
_____e. seizures
_____f. asthma
_____g. chronic headaches
_____h. weight loss

3. EMOTIONAL:
_____a. depressed
_____b. manic
_____c. labile mood
_____d. cries easily
_____e. angry/hostile
_____f. unexpressive of feelings
_____g. inappropriate affect
_____h. passive

4. BEHAVIOR:
_____a. impulsive
_____b. lethargic
_____c. obsessive +/or compulsive
_____d. dangerous risk taking
_____e. self-destructive
_____f. fights verbally
_____g. fist fights

5. SELF-ESTEEM:
_____a. lacks confidence
_____b. overreacts to failure
_____c. poor body image
_____d. poor hygiene
_____e. inappropriate dress
_____f. attention seeking
_____g. substance abuse

Suicide Risk: _____Suicidal Ideations (at present)
                       _____Suicidal Gesture (at present)
                       _____Suicide Attempt
                       _____History of Suicidal Ideation
                       _____History of Attempts
                       When _____
                       How Treated _____

Indicate Level of Dangerousness to Self: Low   Moderate   High
_____Suicidal Statements   _____Drug/Alcohol Involvement
_____Intent   _____Previous Thoughts
_____Means Available   _____Previous Acts
_____Future Oriented   _____Recent Loss(es)
_____Self Mutilating Behavior   _____Knows a person who has
                                       attempted or completed suicide

Interpersonal: Assess Family/Support Systems
List "family members" as stated by client. _____
_____
_____
_____
_____

Indicate family violence. _____
_____
_____

Brief statement of current family relationships (marital, sibling, parent/youth).
_____
_____

List support systems (and coping mechanisms). Include parental or family involvement in religious/civic/volunteer groups, and/or support groups (AA, Alanon, Alateen, etc.).
_____
_____
_____

1. FAMILY:
_____a. frequent verbal arguments
_____b. fist fights
_____c. poor communication
_____d. unclear household rules
_____e. physical abuse
_____f. sexual abuse
_____g. alcohol/drug addiction
_____h. poor parenting skills
_____i. financial problems
_____j. stepparent adjustment problems

2. PEERS:
_____a. gang involvement
_____b. frequent fighting with peers
_____c. no friends

Recent Critical Events in Family:
_____Birth   _____Divorce/Separation   _____Other
_____Death   _____Move
_____Marriage   _____Illness/Hospitalization

1. SCHOOL:
_____a. truancy
_____b. frequent detention
_____c. suspensions; #_____this year
_____d. poor academic performance
_____e. argues with teachers
_____f. does not complete homework
_____g. special education services
_____h. concentration problems

2. COMMUNITY:
_____a. shoplifting
_____b. criminal mischief
_____c. assault
_____d. breaking/entering
_____e. disturbing peace
_____f. robbery
_____g. FWSN
_____h. other delinquent acts
_____i. # police arrests_____
_____j. # court involvements_____

Medical History:
1. Statement of Current Health _____

_____

2. Allergies _____

_____

3. History of medical problems that may relate to presenting problem.

_____

_____

4. List current medications and dosages (include birth control pills).

_____

_____

5. List name and dates of hospitalizations or residential treatment.

_____

_____

Substance Abuse:
1. Type of substance used, quantity, frequency, and duration of use.

_____

_____

Most recent use. _____
2. Sexual Activity: _____Yes _____No
                    _____Multiple Partners
                    _____Use of Protection
                    _____Pregnancies/Abortions
Recommendations: _____

_____

_____

_____

Recommended Referral Resources: _____

_____

_____

_____

Service Provided:
_____Individual Counseling   _____Multiple Agency Contracts
_____Family Counseling   _____Referrer Only
Reason for Non-Admission to Emergency Placement:
_____Request for Crisis Inter. Only ( )   _____Danger to Self/Other ( )
_____Age ( )   _____Criminal Behavior ( )
_____Geographic Area ( )   _____Mentally Retarded ( )
_____Acting Out ( )   _____No Show/No Call Back ( )
_____Physical Handicap ( )   _____Alternate Solution ( )
_____Substance Abuse ( )
Reason for FWSN Recommendation:
_____Runaway   _____Defiant of School Rules
_____Beyond Control   _____Truant
_____Indecent/Immoral Conduct

E — *Examples of Substance Abuse Assessment Instruments*

Family Resources, Inc.

HIGH RISK SCALE

Please answer the following questions about the youth after you have completed his or her assessment.

Section A
1. Is youth residing in a house where parent(s), guardian or other household members have a history of alcohol and/or drug abuse?

Yes_____ No_____

2. Is youth's home located in a community where there is active drug selling or usage?

Yes_____ No_____

3. Has youth been arrested for a drug related offense?

Yes_____ No_____

4. Has anyone in the family ever been arrested for a drug related offense?

Yes_____ No_____

5. Does youth use drugs at least once a week and/or been tested positive within the last three months?

Yes_____ No_____

6. Does youth use drugs more than three times a week?

Yes_____ No_____

7. Has youth ever had a blackout?

Yes_____ No_____

If you answered "yes" to two or more of the above questions, refer to TASC for consideration to enter special services.

Client Name _____ Age_____ Sex_____ Race_____
Program _____
Referring (circle one)   yes   no
Counselor _____
Date completed _____
Address of client _____
_____ Phone _____

Has client dropped out of school? _____

Has client been charged with selling drugs? _____

Recommendations (to be completed after completing Part II - High Risk Assessment):

Counselor _____ Date _____

Supervisor _____ Date _____

What types of drugs have you used? When did you first use? Are you currently using it? How often?

	Yes/No	Using Now Yes/No	When First Tried	Date Last Tried
Alcohol				
Marijuana				
Cocaine/Crack				
LSD/Mushrooms				
Other Hallucinogens				
Inhalants				
Speeds				
Tranquilizers				
Barbiturates				
Over-the-Counter				
Sedatives				
Opiates/Heroin				

Current drug used most often _____
Do you smoke cigarettes? _____
Do you use drugs/alcohol at home with your parents home? _____
Have you increased your drug use in the past year? _____
If yes, when? _____
Have you ever used drugs/alcohol for several days in a row? _____
Have you ever tried to stop using/or cut down your use of drugs/alcohol? _____
Why did you want to stop? _____
Has drugs/alcohol use caused you any problems this past year? _____
If yes, how? _____
Has anyone expressed concern about your use? _____
Does anyone in your home use drugs/alcohol? _____
If yes, who? _____
Do you worry about this person (people)? _____
If yes, why? _____

Recommendations: (To be completed after completing Part II - High Risk Assessment).

Counselor _____ Date _____

Supervisor _____ Date _____

Open-Inn, Inc.

SUBSTANCE ABUSE ASSESSMENT TOOL

Some questions have more than one part. Answer "Yes" even if only one part of the question is yes and others are no.

Section I

Yes No   1. Have you ever been arrested for being in possession of drugs/alcohol or been at a party broken up by police?
___ ___

Yes No   2. Have you ever been suspended from school activities for using drugs/alcohol or skipping classes?
___ ___

Yes No   3. Do you dislike school?
___ ___

Yes No   4. Do you find your family life disappointing or difficult?
___ ___

Yes No   5. Have you stopped participating in extracurricular activities?
___ ___

Yes No   6. Do your friends drink or smoke marijuana?
___ ___

Yes No   7. Have you ever experienced a hangover or a bad trip?
___ ___

Yes No   8. Have you ever lied to your parents about your activities or friends?
___ ___

Yes No   9. Have you made excuses about your or your friends' use of drugs/alcohol?
___ ___

Yes No   10. Do your moods change more than they used to?
___ ___

Yes No   11. Do you think your parents' attitudes are values about drugs and alcohol?
___ ___

Yes No   12. Do you feel as though family activities and religious practices are meaningless to you?
___ ___

Yes No   13. Have your parents ever made excuses for your behaviors to the school, friends, court, other family members?
___ ___

Section II

Yes No 14. Have you ever been arrested for shoplifting, vandalism, driving while
___ ___ intoxicated or possession of drugs/alcohol?

Yes No 15. Have you ever been suspended from school for possession of drug/
___ ___ alcohol or fighting?

Yes No 16. Do you frequently fall asleep in school, have failing grades, truancy,
___ ___ forge passes, excuses about missed school?

Yes No 17. Do you ever take money or objects that can be sold for money from
___ ___ your house?

Yes No 18. Do you ever stay out all night, fight frequently with your parents,
___ ___ spend most of your time at home alone in your room with the door
closed?

Yes No 19. Have you changed your friends from those who do not use drugs/
___ ___ alcohol to those who do?

Yes No 20. Have you lost or gained a lot of weight? Are you less concerned with
___ ___ your personal hygiene than you used to be?

Yes No 21. Do you find it hard to concentrate?
___ ___

Yes No 22. Do you have collapses in memory—times when you could not
___ ___ remember going somewhere or drinking something?

Yes No 23. Do you feel depressed and unworthy?
___ ___

Yes No 24. Have you stopped participating in family activities?
___ ___

Yes No 25. Do you find yourself defending your right to drink or use drugs?
___ ___

Yes No 26. Do you put your family in the position of defending you to school
___ ___ and court for your problems?

Section III

Yes No 27. Have you ever been arrested for robbery, drug dealing, assault and
___ ___ battery, vandalism or prostitution?

Yes No 28. Have you been suspended from school more than once or expelled?

_____ _____

Yes No 29. Have you ever gotten physically violent with your parents or stayed away from home for more than a weekend or left home "for good"?

_____ _____

Yes No 30. Have you ever gotten violent with your friends or started to avoid them?

_____ _____

Yes No 31. Have you ever overdosed, had tremors, dry heaves or a chronic cough?

_____ _____

Yes No 32. Do you blame your parents or friends for your problems?

_____ _____

Yes No 33. Do you explode in anger a lot?

_____ _____

Yes No 34. Are there often times when you cannot remember things you have said or done?

_____ _____

Yes No 35. Have you ever made plans to commit or attempted suicide?

_____ _____

Yes No 36. Do you ever feel paranoid?

_____ _____

Yes No 37. Do you believe in a power greater than yourself?

_____ _____

Yes No 38. Do you turn off when people talk about drugs and alcohol?

_____ _____

Yes No 39. Do you deny having a problem with drugs or alcohol even though you think you do or might?

_____ _____

Yes No 40. Do you think you are endangering your life through your use of drugs/alcohol?

_____ _____

KEY TO SCORING DRUG/ALCOHOL ASSESSMENT

Yes answers in Section I—Stage II.
Yes answers in Section II—Stage III.
Yes answers in Section III—Stage IV.

Samples of Interagency Agreements for Family Resources, Inc.
(formerly Alternative Human Services, Inc.)

Copies of these actual agreements are included for those organizations that wish to develop similar agreements.

CONTENTS

Referral Agreement
Alternative Human Services, Inc.
Youth and Family Connection
and
Sixth Judicial Circuit Court's Psychological Services Unit

I. Purpose

This agreement has been developed between Alternative Human Services' Youth & Family Connection Program (YFC) and Psychological Services Unit of the Sixth Judicial Circuit Court (Juvenile Division), hereinafter referred to as Psychological Services, to promote quality psychological services, consultation and education efforts with programs serving the needs of clients in this circuit.

II. Statement of Agreement

A. Psychological Services agrees to provide the following services to the program.

1. To provide psychological screening and evaluation of youth involved in the Juvenile Justice System and served by YFC when such evaluations are mutually considered to be appropriate.

2. To refer clients to YFC when the staff views such a referral as being appropriate.

3. To adhere to professional standards of confidentiality and to release client information only with properly executed release form signed by client and parent or legal guardian.

4. To accept referrals of clients without regard to race, sex, economic status, color, creed, religion or national origin.

5. To establish adequate liaison services in order to assure coordination of services between the programs.

6. To provide notification to YFC that a client did or did not follow through after being referred. This is simply a yes or no notification and does not violate confidentiality of client contact.

7. To participate in joint training sessions and seminars beneficial to both programs.

B. The Youth & Family Connection (YFC) agrees to provide the following services to the program:

1. To receive referrals from the Psychological Services Unit and to screen these clients for participation in an appropriate Youth & Family Connection program.

2. To adhere to professional standards of confidentiality and to release client information only with properly executed release form signed by client and parent or legal guardian.

3. To establish adequate liaison in order to ensure coordination of services between the programs.
4. To accept referrals of clients without regard to race, sex, economic status, color, creed, religion or national origin.
5. To participate in joint training sessions and seminars beneficial to both agencies.
6. To provide notification to Psychological Services Unit that a client did or did not follow through after being referred. This is simply a yes or no notification and does not violate confidentiality of client contact.

This agreement is entered into by both parties for the stated purpose of providing quality services to youth and their families and may be revised by mutual agreement of both parties. This agreement, upon stated need of either party, may be renegotiated at the end of one year.

_____   _____
Date   Executive Director
                               Alternative Human Services, Inc.
_____
Witness

_____   _____
Date   Director
                               Psychological Services
_____
Witness

Referral Agreement
Alternative Human Services, Inc.
Youth and Family Connection
and
Citizens Dispute Settlement Program

I. Purpose
    This agreement has been developed between Alternative Human Services' Youth & Family Connection Program (YFC) and Citizens Dispute Settlement Program (CDSP) to provide a consistent means of dealing with status offenders and their families by providing Family Crisis Intervention Services (FCI) in Pinellas Country, Florida. The program is designed to meet the need for a coordinated, effective process to assist status offenders and their families at the time of crisis and to assure referrals to appropriate services and agencies.

II. Statement of Agreement
    A. Citizens Dispute Settlement Program (CDSP) agrees to provide the following services to the program.
       1. To refer to another source crisis counseling services to status offenders and their families who are referred from YFC through the Family Crisis Intervention Program.
       2. To accept referrals of clients without regard to race, sex, economic status, color, creed, religion or nation origin.
       3. To adhere to and maintain strict confidentiality of client information and to release such information only with properly executed release form signed by client.
       4. To provide notification to YFC that a client did or did not follow through after being referred to CDSP. This is simply a yes or no notification and does not violate confidentiality of client contact.
       5. To establish and maintain adequate liaison services to assure coordination of services between the two agencies.
    B. The Youth & Family Connection (YFC) agrees to provide the following services to the program:
       1. Provision of crisis intervention counseling at the time of impact to those status offenders, youth and their families seeking assistance.
       2. Provision of short-term shelter services to status offenders for whom this service is deemed necessary.
       3. Provision of short-term shelter (respite care) and counseling services to pre-dependent/delinquent youth for whom these services are deemed appropriate by YFC.

4. Provision of a centralized location for appropriate referral (based upon identification and assessment of need) to an agency of choice, for those families seeking specific types of services.
5. Provision of services to client referred without regard to race, sex, economic status, color, creed, religion or national origin.
6. Maintenance of records of the number of status offenders served by this program and number of status offenders referred to each community agency involved in the Family Crisis Intervention Program.
7. Establishment and maintenance of adequate liaison services to assure coordination of services between the two agencies.
8. Adherence to and maintenance of strict confidentiality of client information and release of such information only with properly executed release form signed by client.

This agreement is entered into by both parties for the stated purpose of providing quality services to status offenders and their families and may be revised by mutual agreement of both parties. This agreement, upon stated need of either party, may be renegotiated at the end of one year.

Date

Witness

Executive Director
Alternative Human Services, Inc.

Date

Witness

Operations Manager
Citizens Dispute Settlement Program

Referral Agreement
Alternative Human Services, Inc.
Youth and Family Connection
and
Florida State Department of Health and Rehabilitative Services

I. Purpose

This agreement has been developed between Alternative Human Services' Youth & Family Connection Program (YFC) and Florida State Department of Health and Rehabilitative Services (DHRS), to provide a consistent means of dealing with Families in Need of Services (FINS) by providing Family Crisis Intervention Services (FCI) in Pinellas County, Florida. The program is designed to meet the need for a coordinated, effective process to assist Children in Need of Services (CINS) and their families at the time of crisis and to assure referrals to appropriate services and agencies.

II. Statement of Agreement

A. Florida State Department of Health and Rehabilitative Services (DHRS), agrees to provide the following services to the program:

1. To provide initial assessment services to all FINS/CINS and pre-dependent youth and their families who seek assistance through DHRS Intake Units, Protective Investigation, Delinquency/FINS/CINS.

2. To accept referrals of clients without regard to race, sex, economic status, color, creed, religion or national origin.

3. To establish and maintain adequate liaison services to assure coordination of services between the two agencies.

4. To refer those FINS/CINS and pre-dependent youth to YFC who are not adjudicated delinquent or dependent.

5. To provide notification to YFC that a client did or did not follow through after being referred to DHRS. This is simply a yes or no notification and does not violate confidentiality of client contact.

B. The Youth & Family Connection (YFC) agrees to provide the following services to the program:

1. Provision of crisis intervention counseling at the time of impact to those CINS youth and their families seeking assistance from the Florida State DHRS Delinquency -FINS/CINS Intake Units.

2. Provision of short-term shelter and counseling to Families in Need of Services that are deemed appropriate by YFC.

3. Provision of a centralized location for appropriate referral (based upon identification and assessment of need) to an agency of choice, for those families seeking specific types of services.

4. Provision of services to client referred without regard to race, sex, economic status, color, creed, religion or national origin.
5. Maintenance of records of the number of Families in Need of Services served by this program and number of Families in Need of Services referred to each community agency involved in the Family Crisis Intervention Program.
6. Establishment and maintenance of adequate liaison services to assure coordination of services between the two agencies.
7. Adherence to and maintenance of strict confidentiality of client information and release of such information only with properly executed release form signed by client.
8. To provide short-term shelter (respite care) as these services are deemed appropriate by YFC.
9. To refer to Florida Abuse Registry any youths who are alleged to have been abused or neglected.

This agreement is entered into by both parties for the stated purpose of providing quality services to status offenders and their families and may be revised by mutual agreement of both parties. This agreement, upon stated need of either party, may be renegotiated at the end of one (1) year.

Date	Executive Director
	Alternative Human Services, Inc.
Witness	

Date	District Administrator
	Florida State Department of Health and
Witness	Rehabilitative Services, District V

Referral Agreement
Alternative Human Services, Inc.
Youth and Family Connection
and
Directions for Mental Health, Inc.

I. Purpose

This agreement has been developed between Alternative Human Services' Youth & Family Connection Program (YFC) and Directions for Mental Health, Inc., (Directions), to provide a consistent means of dealing with status offenders and their families by providing Family Crisis Intervention Services (FCI) in Pinellas County, Florida. The program is designed to meet the need for a coordinated, effective process to assist status offenders and their families at the time of crisis and to assure referrals to appropriate services and agencies.

II. Statement of Agreement

A. Directions for Mental Health, Inc. (Directions), agrees to provide the following services to the program:

1. To provide the full range of out-patient mental health services to status offenders and their families who are referred from YFC through the Family Crisis Intervention Program and deemed appropriate by Directions.

2. To schedule, within forty-eight (48) hours, families referred by AHS-YFC who are in immediate crisis. These calls should be channeled through the Supervisor of Children's Services at each of the Directions locations offering these services as they can expedite service delivery:

   a. 8823-115 Ave. North
      Largo, Florida 34643
      Supervisor
      Phone: 393-1600

   b. 2280 U.S. 19 North, Suite 139
      Clearwater, Florida 34622
      Supervisor
      Phone: 536-5950

   c. 1700 U.S. 19 South, Suite 11
      Tarpon Springs, Florida 34689
      Supervisor
      Phone: 937-7715

3. To accept referrals of clients without regard to race, sex, economic status, color, creed, religion or national origin.

4. To provide aftercare family counseling services to eligible former clients of YFC through routine referrals.
5. To provide notification to YFC that a client did or did not follow through after being referred to Directions. This is simply a yes or no notification and does not violate confidentiality of client contact.
6. To adhere to and maintain strict confidentiality of client information and to release such information only with properly executed release form signed by client.
7. To establish and maintain adequate liaison services to assure coordination of services between the two agencies.

B. The Youth & Family Connection (YFC) agrees to provide the following services to the program:

1. Provision of crisis intervention counseling at the time of impact to those status offenders, youth and their families seeking assistance.
2. Provision of short-term shelter services to status offenders for whom this service is deemed necessary.
3. Provision of a centralized location for appropriate referral (based upon identification and assessment of need) to an agency of choice, for those families seeking specific types of services.
4. Provision of services to client referred without regard to race, sex, economic status, color, creed, religion or national origin.
5. Maintenance of records of the number of status offenders served by this program and number of status offenders referred to each community agency involved in the Family Crisis Intervention Program.
6. Establishment and maintenance of adequate liaison services to assure coordination of services between the two agencies.
7. Adherence to and maintenance of strict confidentiality of client information and release of such information only with properly executed release form signed by client.

This agreement is entered into by both parties for the stated purpose of providing quality services to status offenders and their families and may be revised by mutual agreement of both parties or may be terminated by either party, after giving thirty (30) days written notice to the other party. All fees for services will be charged according to the Directions Fee Schedule. Families utilizing Directions' services will be responsible for fees incurred. AHS-YFC will not be responsible for fees incurred by families referred by AHS-YFC. Any administrative problems which may arise in relation to this agreement shall be addressed at the appropriate administrative level by representatives designated for that purpose by the parties to this agreement. This agreement will be renegotiated at the end of one (1) year.

_____   _____
Date   Executive Director
                                     Alternative Human Services, Inc.
_____
Witness

_____   _____
Date   Executive Director
                                     Directions for Mental Health, Inc.
_____
Witness

Referral Agreement
Alternative Human Services, Inc.
Youth and Family Connection
and
Family Service Centers

I. Purpose
This agreement has been developed between Alternative Human Services' Youth & Family Connection Program (YFC) and Family Service Centers (FSC) to provide a consistent means of dealing with status offenders and their families by providing Family Crisis Intervention Services (FCI) in Pinellas County, Florida. The program is designed to meet the need for a coordinated, effective process to assist status offenders and their families at the time of crisis and to assure referrals to appropriate services and agencies.

II. Statement of Agreement
A. Family Service Centers (FSC) agrees to provide the following services to the program.
   1. To provide family counseling services to status offenders and their families who are referred from YFC through the Family Crisis Intervention Program.
   2. To assign a counselor at its Seminole office for one hour each week to provide family counseling services to status offenders and their families referred by YFC through the Family Crisis Intervention Program.
   3. To assign a counselor at its Clearwater office for one hour each week to provide family counseling services to status offenders and their families referred by YFC through the Family Crisis Intervention Program.
   4. To assign a counselor at its Palm Harbor office for one hour each week to provide family counseling services to status offenders and their families referred by YFC through the Family Crisis Intervention Program.
   5. Appointments for the initial family counseling service may be made by calling the intake counselor in the office where the appointment is to be arranged.
   6. Fees for family counseling services at Family Service Centers are determined individually with each family, and are based on ability to pay. No family will be denied service because of inability to pay.
   7. To accept referrals of clients without regard to race, sex, economic status, color, creed, religion or national origin.

8. Status offenders and their families may also be eligible for other services provided by FSC. These services include: Family Life Education, Single Parent Services, Homemaker Service, Sexual Assault Services and Travelers' Aide.
9. To provide notification to YFC that a client did or did not follow through after being referred to FSC. This is simply a yes or no notification and does not violate confidentiality of client contact.
10. To provide aftercare family counseling services to eligible former clients of YFC through routine referrals.
11. To participate in joint staff training activities deemed necessary and beneficial to both agencies.

B. Alternative Human Services' Youth & Family Connection (YFC) agrees to provide the following services to the program:
1. Provision of crisis intervention counseling at the time of impact to those status offenders, youth and their families seeking assistance.
2. Provision of short-term shelter services to status offenders for whom this service is deemed necessary.
3. Provision of a centralized location for appropriate referral (based upon identification and assessment of need) to an agency of choice, for those families seeking specific types of services.
4. Provision of services to client referred without regard to race, sex, economic status, color, creed, religion or national origin.
5. Maintenance of records of the number of status offenders served by this program and number of status offenders referred to each community agency involved in the Family Crisis Intervention Program.
6. Establishment and maintenance of adequate liaison services to assure coordination of services between the two agencies.
7. Adherence to and maintenance of strict confidentiality of client information and release of such information only with properly executed release form signed by client.
8. Participation in joint staff training activities deemed necessary and beneficial to both agencies.

This agreement is entered into by both parties for the stated purpose of providing quality services to status offenders and their families and may be revised by mutual agreement of both parties. This agreement, upon stated need of either party, may be renegotiated at the end of one year.

Date _____   Executive Director
                                Alternative Human Services, Inc.

Witness _____

Date _____   Executive Director
                                Family Service Centers, Inc.

Witness _____

Referral Agreement
Alternative Human Services, Inc.
and
Gulf Coast Jewish Family Service, Inc.
Adopt-A-Grandchild Program

I. Purpose

This agreement has been developed between Alternative Human Services Youth and Gulf Coast Jewish Family Service, Inc., (GCJFS), Adopt-A-Grandchild Program, to ensure effective and expedient communication between the provider agency, GCJFS, and relevant referral agencies in order that children, families, and senior citizens receive quality services in the most appropriate and least problematic manner available.

II. Statement of Agreement

A. Gulf Coast Jewish Family Service, Inc., (GCJFS), agrees to provide the following services to the program:

1. To assure that the provision of support and mental health services including, but not limited to, the matching of children and senior citizens residing in Pinellas Country and that individual, group, and family counseling services are available, accessible and acceptable, reflecting quality, cost effectiveness and continuity of client care.

2. To provide priority placements to children and individuals in greatest need of support services and provide continuity of care services to those clients.

3. To receive clients without regard to race, sex, economic status, color, creed, religion, national origin or physical handicap.

4. Coordinate services and refer clients who meet admission criteria with other pertinent human services within the service area, and those significant ones outside the area, to assure that the total needs of the client are met in as comprehensive a manner as is possible.

5. To verbally provide client referral information for all purposes of expeditious continuity of care services, while assuring safeguards to current standards of client confidentiality. Written correspondence will be exchanged only with properly executed Releases of Information signed by the client, or if the client is under 18, the client's parent or guardian.

    6. To provide adequate liaison and coordination to ensure adequate staff contact, referral coordination and general information sharing.

    7. To maintain responsibility for continuity of care for clients within and among all program elements of the Center and provide movement from one program to another with as few obstacles and as little interruption in the clients' therapeutic regime as possible.

    8. To provide statistical reports for research or administrative purposes as may be required by GCJFS Administration, the Juvenile Welfare Board, United Way, or any other funding source.

    9. To develop an individual Service Plan for each client and implement the Plan over the course of the service.

    10. To maintain an individual case record for each client served.

    11. To maintain written screening and intake procedures.

B. Alternative Human Services, Inc. (AHS) agrees to provide the following services to the program:

    1. Assurance that the provision of mental health evaluation and treatment services are available, accessible and acceptable, reflecting quality and continuity of care.

    2. Receive clients without regard to race, sex, economic status, color, creed, religion, national origin or physical handicap.

    3. Provision of referral for clients who meet admission criteria with other pertinent human services within the service area, and those significant ones outside the area, to assure that the total needs of the client are met in as comprehensive manner as is possible.

    4. To verbally provide client referral information for purposes of expeditious continuity of care services, while assuring safeguards to current standards of client confidentiality. Written correspondence will be exchanged only with properly executed Releases of Information signed by the client, or if the client is under age 18, the client's parent or guardian.

    5. Maintenance of case plans and records on each client served.

    6. Provision of statistical information for research or administrative reporting purposes as needed.

III. In conclusion, GCJFS and Alternative Human Services, Inc. agree:

A. To review requests for service in a timely manner and to process such requests when agreed upon by both agencies.

B. This Agreement shall be effective from date of signature through the calendar year, and will be reviewed and/or renewed on an annual basis.

_____   _____
Date   Executive Director
                                                                        Alternative Human Services, Inc.
_____
Witness

_____   _____
Date   Executive Director
                                                                        Gulf Coast Jewish Family Service, Inc.
_____
Witness

Referral Agreement
Alternative Human Services, Inc.
Youth and Family Connection
and
Marriage and Family Counseling of Pinellas, Inc.

I. Purpose

    This agreement has been developed between Alternative Human Services' Youth & Family Connection Program (YFC) and Marriage & Family Counseling of Pinellas, Inc., (M&FC), to provide a consistent means of dealing with status offenders and their families by providing Family Crisis Intervention Services (FCI) in Pinellas County, Florida. The program is designed to meet the need for a coordinated, effective process to assist status offenders and their families at the time of crisis and to assure referrals to appropriate services and agencies.

II. Statement of Agreement

    A. Marriage and Family Counseling of Pinellas, Inc. (M&FC), agrees to provide the following services to the program.

       1. To provide crisis counseling services to status offenders and their families who are referred from YFC through the Family Crisis Intervention Program.

       2. To provide one slotted appointment time per week at both its St. Petersburg and Clearwater office to serve referrals from YFC as part of the Family Crisis Intervention service.

       3. To accept referrals of clients without regard to race, sex, economic status, color, creed, religion, national origin.

       4. Status offenders and their families may also be eligible for other services provided by M&FC. These services include: parenting classes, couple communication classes, group counseling, individual counseling and premarital counseling.

       5. To provide notification to YFC that a client did or did not follow through after being referred to M&FC. This is simply a yes or no notification and does not violate confidentiality of client contact.

       6. To provide aftercare family counseling services to eligible former clients of YFC through routine referrals.

    B. The Youth & Family Connection (YFC) agrees to provide the following services to the program:

       1. Provision of crisis intervention counseling at the time of impact to those status offenders, youth and their families seeking assistance.

2. Provision of short-term shelter services to status offenders for whom this service is deemed necessary.
3. Provision of a centralized location for appropriate referral (based upon identification and assessment of need) to an agency of choice, for those families seeking specific types of services.
4, Provision of services to client referred without regard to race, sex, economic status, color, creed, religion or national origin.
5. Maintenance of records of the number of status offenders served by this program and number of status offenders referred to each community agency involved in the Family Crisis Intervention Program.
6. Establishment and maintenance of adequate liaison services to assure coordination of services between the two agencies.
7. Adherence to and maintenance of strict confidentiality of client information and release of such information only with properly executed release form signed by client.

This agreement is entered into by both parties for the stated purpose of providing quality services to status offenders and their families and may be revised by mutual agreement of both parties. This agreement, upon stated need of either party, may be renegotiated at the end of one (1) year.

_____
Date

_____
Witness

Executive Director
Alternative Human Services, Inc.

_____
Date

_____
Witness

Executive Director
Marriage and Family Counseling of Pinellas, Inc.

Referral Agreement
Alternative Human Services, Inc.
Youth and Family Connection
and
Mental Health Association of Pinellas County, Inc.
(Project Together)

I. Purpose
    This agreement has been developed between Alternative Human Services' Youth & Family connection Program (YFC) and Mental Health Association of Pinellas County, Inc., Project Together.

II. Statement of Agreement
    A. The two parties involved agree to the following provisions:
       1. Supply current information regarding the nature of services, types of clients served, eligibility requirements and availability of services to each other's facility.
       2. Make referrals of appropriate clients/members, in accordance with #1 above, by the pre-arranged processes.
       3. Supply appropriate and relevant information on the referred client/member. Said information shall include, but not be limited to, the following: name, address, telephone number, and reason for referral.
       4. Upon receipt of information on a referred client/member, shall provide an appointment time and date when the referred client/member can be seen.
       5. Accept and process the referral to determine the eligibility and appropriateness for services.
       6. If requested, provide referring agency with oral and/or written reports on the treatment progress of the referred client/member (with appropriate signed releases from client/member).
       7. Participate, when appropriate, in the joint staff meetings and conferences on "in-common" clients/members.

This agreement is entered into by both parties for the stated purpose of providing quality services to clients/members and their families and may be revised by mutual agreement of both parties. This agreement, upon stated need of either party, may be renegotiated at the end of one year.

_____   _____
Date   Executive Director
                                         Alternative Human Services, Inc.
_____
Witness

_____   _____
Date   Executive Director
                                         Mental Health Association of Pinellas
_____   County, Inc.
Witness

Referral Agreement
Alternative Human Services, Inc.
Youth and Family Connection
and
Suncoast Center for Community Mental Health, Inc.

I. Purpose

This agreement has been developed between Alternative Human Services' Youth & Family Connection Program (YFC) and Suncoast Center for Community Mental Health, Inc. (Suncoast Center) to provide a consistent means of dealing with status offenders and their families by providing Family Crisis Intervention Services (FCI) in Pinellas County, Florida. The program is designed to meet the need for a coordinated, effective process to assist status offenders and their families at the time of crisis and to assure referrals to appropriate services and agencies.

II. Statement of Agreement

A. Suncoast Center for Community Mental Health agrees to provide the following services to the program.

1. To provide the full range of outpatient mental health services to status offenders and their families who are referred from YFC through the Family Crisis Intervention Program and CINS/FINS Program deemed appropriate by the Suncoast Center.

2. To provide aftercare family counseling services to eligible former clients of YFC and CINS/FINS through routine referrals.

3. To accept referrals of clients without regard to race, sex, economic status, color, creed, religion or national origin.

4. To adhere to and maintain strict confidentiality of client information and to release such information only with properly executed release form signed by client.

5. To provide notification to YFC and CINS/FINS that a client did or did not follow through after being referred to Suncoast Center. This is simply a yes or no notification and does not violate confidentiality of client contact.

6. To establish and maintain adequate liaison services to assure coordination of services between the two agencies.

7. To provide specialized mental health psychological and related evaluations, and consultation and treatment service for clients of Alternative Human Services' Youth & Family Connection and CINS/FINS Programs.

B. The Youth & Family Connection (YFC) agrees to provide the following services to the program.

1. Provision of crisis intervention counseling at the time of impact to those status offenders, youth and their families seeking assistance.
2. Provision of short-term shelter services to status offenders for whom this service is deemed necessary.
3. Provision of a centralized location for appropriate referral (based upon identification and assessment of need) to an agency of choice, for those families seeking specific types of services.
4. Provision of services to client referred without regard to race, sex, economic status, color, creed, religion or national origin.
5. Maintenance of records of the number of status offenders served by this program and number of status offenders referred to each community agency involved in the Family Crisis Intervention Program.
6. Establishment and maintenance of adequate liaison services to assure coordination of services between the two agencies.
7. Adherence to and maintenance of strict confidentiality of client information and release of such information only with properly executed release form signed by client.
8. Provision of non-emergency, short-term shelter services (respite care) for clients of the Suncoast Center's Homebased Intensive Family Services. Such clients need not be status offenders, and will not present needs or demands that exceed the capabilities or compromise the Program objectives of the YFC runaway shelters.
9. Referral of CINS/FINS youth and their families to Suncoast Center for evaluation of treatment of mental health problems.

This agreement is entered into by both parties for the stated purpose of providing quality services to status offenders, clients of Suncoast Center's Homebase Intensive Family Services and their families. It shall be effective until such time as changes are desired by either party. Each agency will review the agreement annually. If amendments are needed, appropriate staff of each agency will agree to meet within a reasonable time period and will work toward a problem resolution. Then, a new agreement will be drawn up and signed by the executive directors. Either Suncoast Center or YFC may terminate the agreement upon thirty (30) days' written notice to the other party.

Date

Witness

Executive Director
Alternative Human Services, Inc.

Date

Witness

Executive Director
Suncoast Center for Community Mental Health, Inc.

Review of Agreement between SUNCOAST CENTER FOR COMMUNITY MENTAL HEALTH, INC., and Alternative Human Services Youth and Family Connection

Date _____ Changes: Yes_____ No_____

_____
Executive Director
Suncoast Center for Community Mental Health, Inc.

Date _____ Changes: Yes_____ No_____

_____
Executive Director
Suncoast Center for Community Mental Health, Inc.

Date _____ Changes: Yes_____ No_____

_____
Executive Director
Suncoast Center for Community Mental Health, Inc.

Date _____ Changes: Yes_____ No_____

_____
Executive Director
Suncoast Center for Community Mental Health, Inc.

Date _____ Changes: Yes_____ No_____

_____
Executive Director
Suncoast Center for Community Mental Health, Inc.

Date _____ Changes: Yes_____ No_____

_____
Executive Director
Suncoast Center for Community Mental Health, Inc.

Referral Agreement
Alternative Human Services, Inc.
Youth and Family Connection
and
YWCA Project Help Program

I. Purpose

This agreement has been developed between Alternative Human Services' Youth & Family Connection Program (YFC) and YWCA Project Help Program (Project Help) to provide a consistent means of dealing with status offenders and their families by providing Family Crisis Intervention Services (FCI) in Pinellas County, Florida. The program is designed to meet the need for a coordinated, effective process to assist status offenders and their families at the time of crisis and to assure referrals to appropriate services and agencies.

II. Statement of Agreement

A. Project Help agrees to provide the following services to the program.

1. To provide crisis counseling services to status offenders and their families who are referred from YFC through the Family Crisis Intervention Program.

2. To make appointments for referrals from the Family Crisis Intervention Program within a maximum of two (2) days after referrals are phoned into the program.

3. To provide appropriate aftercare services to eligible clients of YFC through routine referrals.

4. To provide a full range of services to pregnant adolescents and their families as deemed appropriate by Project Help or youth who may be eligible for other services provided by Project Help. These services include: Family Life Education, early intervention and pregnancy counseling, academic education, child care, health care coordination to teenage families, and counseling related to sexual issues for teenage males.

5. To charge no fees for counseling. Fees for other services are based on ability to pay. No family will be denied service because of inability to pay.

6. To accept referrals of clients without regard to race, sex, economic status, color, creed, religion or national origin.

7. To adhere to and maintain strict confidentiality of client information and to release such information only with properly executed release form signed by client.

8. To provide notification to YFC that a client did or did not follow through after being referred to Project Help. This is simply a yes or no notification and does not violate confidentiality of client contact.
9. To establish and maintain adequate liaison services to assure coordination of services between the two agencies.

B. The Youth & Family Connection (YFC) agrees to provide the following services to the program:

1. Provision of crisis intervention counseling at no cost at the time of impact to those status offenders, youth and their families seeking assistance.
2. Provision of short-term shelter services to status offenders for whom this service is deemed necessary.
3. Provision of a centralized location for appropriate referral (based upon identification and assessment of need) to an agency of choice, for those families seeking specific types of services.
4. Provision of services to client referred without regard to race, sex, economic status, color, creed, religion or national origin.
5. Maintenance of records of the number of status offenders served by this program and number of status offenders referred to each community agency involved in the Family Crisis Intervention Program.
6. Establishment and maintenance of adequate liaison services to assure coordination of services between the two agencies.
7. Adherence to and maintenance of strict confidentiality of client information and release of such information only with properly executed release form signed by client.

This agreement is entered into by both parties for the stated purpose of providing quality services to status offenders and their families and may be revised by mutual agreement of both parties. This agreement, upon stated need of either party, may be renegotiated at the end of one (1) year.

Date   Executive Director
                                                    Alternative Human Services, Inc.

Witness

Date   Executive Director
                                                    YWCA of St. Petersburg

Witness

Referral Agreement
Alternative Human Services, Inc.
Youth and Family Connection
and
The Pinellas County Sheriff's Department

I. Purpose

This agreement has been developed between Alternative Human Services' Youth & Family Connection Program (YFC) and The Pinellas County Sheriff's Department to provide a consistent means of dealing with status offenders and their families by YFC providing short term residential counseling services to appropriate youth. The program is designed to meet the need for a coordinated, effective process to assist status offenders and their families at the time of crisis and to assure referrals to appropriate services and referrals.

II. Statement of Agreement

A. Sheriff's Department agrees to provide the following services to the program.

1. To try to locate parents (guardians or legal custodian) of youth in sheriff's custody for status offense or non-person, non-violent misdemeanors.

2. To establish and maintain adequate liaison services to assure coordination of services between the two agencies.

3. To refer those youth and their families with status offense behaviors or those who are not adjudicated delinquent or dependent.

4. Once youth is placed in shelter by Sheriff's Department, The Sheriff's Department will continue to try to locate and contact a responsible adult of the youth and keep the shelter informed of its efforts hourly.

5. To pick youth up if no longer deemed appropriate for shelter services and transport to youth's home, HRS or JDC.

B. Alternative Human Services Youth & Family Connection (YFC) agrees to provide the following services to the program:

1. Provision of crisis intervention counseling at the time of impact to those status offenders, youth and their families referred for assistance.

2. Provision of short-term shelter and counseling services to status offenders, and non-person, non-violent misdemeanants that are deemed appropriate by YFC.

3. Provision of services to clients referred without regard to race, sex, economic status, color, creed, religion, or national origin.

4. Establishment and maintenance of adequate liaison services to assure coordination of services between the two agencies.
5. Adherence to and maintenance of strict confidentiality of client information and release of such information only with properly executed release form signed by client parent or legal guardian.
6. To contact the Sheriff's Department if any of their referrals leave the shelter prior to being picked up by a parent or legal guardian.

This agreement is entered into by both parties for the stated purpose of providing quality services to status offenders and their families and may be revised by mutual agreement of both parties. This agreement, upon stated need of either party, may be renegotiated at the end of one year.

Date

Witness

Date

Witness

Executive Director
Alternative Human Services, Inc.

Sheriff Everett Rice
Sheriff's Department

Agreement
Family Resources, Inc.
and
Operation Par, Inc.

I. Purpose

This agreement has been developed between Family Resources, Inc., a private, non-profit agency for its Outreach Programs, hereinafter referred to as PAR, in an effort to provide services to runaway youth and their families.

II. Statement of Agreement

A. FR agrees to the following:

1. To provide outreach services to runaway youth and their families in Pinellas County in order to prevent and reduce illegal alcohol and other drug use.
2. To refer families to PAR for substance abuse assessment, education programs and peer support groups.
3. To maintain regular contacts with PAR to assure proper coordination of services.
4. To refer clients without regard to race, sex, sexual preference, economic status, color, creed, religion, national origin or physical handicap.
5. To mention the association of FR and PAR's cooperative efforts when/where appropriate.
6. To pay PAR $2,100 monthly (monthly billing) for the period October 1, 1991–September 30, 1992.
7. To submit one copy of relevant quarterly reports to PAR.
8. To provide follow up and outreach on appropriate referrals from PAR on high risk youth who have failed to appear for substance abuse assessments.
9. To identify a contact person within the agency to facilitate interagency communication relative to this agreement.

B. PAR agrees to the following:

1. To provide substance abuse assessments and appropriate referrals as soon as possible when requested by the FR counselors.
2. To provide, as appropriate, parent survival courses without charge to the client.
3. To provide, as appropriate, youth early intervention schools and adolescent topic groups.
4. To provide training for FR staff on adolescent substance abuse issues, identification, assessment, and prevention and education curriculum.

5. To provide on-site clinical consultation pertaining to alcohol and other drug screening by FR staff.
6. To attend FR case consultations to provide input regarding substance abuse issues as appropriate.
7. To work with FR clinical staff through the Outclient Quality Assurance team to assist with the development of Quality Assurance indicators that address clinical measures and their link to substance abuse issues.
8. To provide a specified contact person within PAR for this agreement.
9. To assist with a FR staff training needs assessment and training plan relative to substance abuse issues.
10. To maintain regular contacts with outreach staff to assure proper coordination of services.
11. To accept referrals from FR without regard to race, sex, sexual preference, economic status, color, creed, religion, national origin or physical handicap.
12. To accept referrals from FR outreach as priority referrals relative to any current or future waiting lists for the services outlined in this agreement.
13. To provide routine feedback to the referral agent as to whether or not the client followed through with referrals and the status of the case.
14. To submit an invoice for $2,100 monthly to FR.
15. To identify a contact person within the agency to facilitate interagency communication relative to this agreement.

Confidentiality:
1. Family Resources and Operation PAR acknowledge that in receiving, storing, processing, or otherwise dealing with any patient/client or patient/client information from clients of each other, are fully bound by the Federal confidentiality regulations, "Confidentiality of Alcohol and Drug Abuse Patient Records," 42 CFR Part 2, dated June 9, 1987. "Records" means any information whether recorded or not relating to a patient/client received or acquired by a Federally assisted alcohol or drug program.
2. If necessary, will resist in judicial proceedings any efforts to obtain access to patient/client records except as permitted by 42 CFR Part 2.
3. Will not redisclose patient/client identifying information except that Family Resources and PAR may disclose patient/client iden-

tifying information obtained under this agreement back to each other.

Confidentiality Protection:

This agreement extends in full the protection of 42 CFR Part 2 to Family Resources, Inc. and all past, present, and future employees who may have or gain access to confidential patient/client information collected under this agreement.

This agreement is entered into by both parties for the stated purpose of reducing and preventing the illegal use of alcohol and other drugs among of runaway youth and may be revised by mutual written agreement of both parties. It is understood by both parties that funding changes may necessitate an immediate revision of this agreement. This agreement is in effect until June 30, 1992 unless otherwise modified by both parties, is subject to the availability of funds and may be terminated with 24 hours notice by either party.

_____   _____
Family Resources, Inc.   Operation PAR, Inc.

_____   _____
Date   Date

G

Client Log, Community Contact Log, and Data Collection Form

NASW Demonstration Project
Quarterly Report—September 30, 1991

OUTREACH WORKER LOG

Outreach Worker _____ Month _____

Date	Time Spent	Contact Mode	TGP	Contact/Address	Telephone Number	Outcome/Follow-up

NASW Demonstration Project
Quarterly Report—September 30, 1991

COMMUNITY PRESENTATION

Date	Topic/Presentor	Location	# Youth

NASW Demonstration Project
Quarterly Report—September 30, 1991

OUTREACH WORKER CLIENT DATA FORM

Client Name _____ Client # _____

Address _____

_____

School _____

Phone # _____ Age_____ Race_____ Sex_____

Family Type _____ # in Family _____ Income _____ Grade _____

Referred by _____ Date _____

Date/Location/Time Initial Contact w/Client

Date _____ Location _____ Time _____

Adults Seen _____ Siblings Seen & Ages _____

Assessment of client/family needs

Referrals Made by Outreach Worker

Agency	Date	Phone #	Rel.	A,B,C

Additional Comments: _____

_____

Termination Date_____   _____
                                      Outreach Worker Signature

Parents interested in having their children participate in the Outreach Program are asked to sign below.

I, hereby release Family Resources, Inc. to use information gathered from follow-up telephone calls or letters, from any liability. It is my understanding that this information will be kept strictly confidential and used for statistical and funding purposes only.

_____   _____
Parent   Telephone #

_____   _____
Youth's Name   Date

Index